Raising Happy Toddlers

How to Build Great Parenting Skills and Stop Yelling at Your Kids

by
Celia Kibler

Published Proudly in the United States of America
Copyright ©Celia Kibler 2021

All rights reserved.

This book cannot be copied, resold or redistributed without prior consent of its author.

Copyright ©Celia Kibler 2021

ALL RIGHTS RESERVED. No part of this book, or its associated ancillary materials may be reproduced or transmitted in any form or by any means, electronic or mechanical, including photocopying, recording, or by any informational storage or retrieval system without permission from the publisher.

Cover design by Justin Cappon Pro

For publishing consideration:
celia@celiakibler.com

"I believe the children are our future.
Teach them well
& let them lead the way.
Show them all the beauty
they possess inside.
Give them a sense of pride
to make it easier.
Let the children's laughter,
remind us how we used to be."

"The Greatest Love of All"
Lyrics by Linda Creed
Music by Michael Masser
Recorded by
George Benson (1977)
Whitney Houston (1984)

I dedicate this book to my kids, all of them.

The blessings I gave birth to and the blessings I gained through my 2nd marriage.

Lauren, our only girl and my first child. We grew up together. You've always been there for me, my sounding board, my joy, my beauty (inside and out). You were the first guinea pig for all of my parenting methods (it worked out pretty well... except for that fish thing). You are an amazing Mom. You fill your home with love, energy, kindness and fun. You are the daughter I've always dreamed of, a constant joy in my life. I am so blessed and honored to be your Mom.

Kyle, our son and my last baby I gave birth to. You are filled with kindness, warmth and so much love. Your sense of humor is second to none. You have made me laugh so hard I'd cry. Every minute I spend with you is so precious to me and I am forever grateful that God chose me to be your Mom. You will always be my superhero.

Ryan, our oldest that I did not give birth to. You lived with us the longest, you called me Mom and you took me on a journey that we both would grow and blossom from. You are an amazing Dad, who loves your children unconditionally. I am eternally grateful that you are my son and that we've shared this road of life. You make me proud each and every day.

Paul, our middle child that I did not give birth to. You are filled with more love than most people I know. Your heart is as big as the moon. You are always there to help and care for people that come into your life. You are a great Dad and I am endlessly proud to call you my son.

Ross, our youngest that I did not give birth to. You are now a new Dad and I am so very proud of you. You have grown to be strong, independent, determined and hard working. You're smart, funny and full of love and I am so grateful and honored that I get to be your Mom.

The five of you are the inspiration for this book. You have given me the life experience to help others. You have taken me on the wildest, most fun ride of my life and I love all of you now and forever. You complete me.

To my **Grandchildren**, you are a testament that good, intentional parenting continues to affect this world for generations to come. I love you all. You put the sparkle in your Gamon's eyes and heart.

To my husband **Rock**, who has always believed in me, supported me and stuck with me through the ups and downs. This would not have been possible without you. I love you.

To my Dad & Mom, you planted in me the seeds that have made me who I am today, and I am forever grateful. I love you both and you will always live in my heart.

To my clients, my students and all the children that fill my life each and every day, to say I am blessed is an understatement. You have allowed me to live my dream. Your success has given me the confidence in my work, techniques and my ability to pursue my passion of impacting the lives of parents and children for the better.

To you, my reader, I am grateful that you have chosen my book to guide you on your journey. I hope the words within become the voices in your head as you guide your children on their journey into adulthood.

Let's all join together to create a world of children that blossom from their childhoods and create a future that all of us can be proud of!

TABLE OF CONTENTS

READ THIS FIRST

SECTION 1: CREATING FAMILY HARMONY

1. Becoming a Pro-Active Parent 20
2. Parenting on the Same Page 26
3. Being their Role Model 33
4. The Family Meeting 37
5. Working Parents: Finding Balance 44
6. Siblings: Calming the Chaos 50
7. Your Growing Family: Introducing a
   New Baby 59
8. Special Kids, Special Love 64
9. Patience: Taming the Storm 72

SECTION 2: COMMUNICATION & ATTITUDE

10. Communication: Where It All Begins 74
11. Who's in Charge Here? 79
12. Creating a Kind, Nice Child 82
13. Gratitude: Changing your 'tude 86
14. When Your Child Stops Listening 95
15. One & Done or "If I don't yell, they
    don't listen!" 101
16. When Children Bend the Truth and Lie 108
17. Talking Back: The Symptom of Growing
    Independence 116

SECTION 3: FUN & LEARNING

18. Play: It's Not Just a Game,
    It's an Education 120
19. Reading: The Gateway to Language 126
20. Social Life: Discovering a World Outside
    of Their Own... 131
21. Building Character: Five Important
    Life Hacks...136
22. Schools & Day Cares: Separating from
    Your Child.. 143

SECTION 4: BEHAVIOR & RESPONSIBILITY

23. Consistency: The Key to Good
    Parenting & Breaking Habits 152
24. Empowerment & Independence 157
25. Mastering Schedules & Routines 161
26. Boundaries: The Key to Feeling Safe,
    Secure & Loved.. 167
27. Consequences: The Result of Choice................ 171
28. Instant Gratification vs. Delayed
    Gratification.. 178
29. Chores: Making them Fun for Everyone,
    even Toddlers 184
30. "I'm Bored": Those Dreaded Words
    & Overuse of Electronics 189

SECTION 5: TRIALS & TRIBULATIONS

31. The Picky Eater 196
32. Screen Time on Your Time............................. 205
33. Tattling vs. Telling.. 209
34. Why?: The Most Aggravating Word in a Toddler's Vocabulary................................ 213
35. Taming the Tantrums...................................... 218
36. Aggression: Taming the Monster Within 224
37. Potty Training 232
38. Breaking the Habit: Pacifiers, Bottles, etc. 240
39. Sleep: Making it Happen................................. 247
40. It's Time to Talk About it: Opening Up About Difficult Topics...................................... 254

IT'S JUST THE BEGINNING

CONTINUE YOUR JOURNEY... YOU'RE ONE SHIFT AWAY

Join the BeABetterParent.com Membership & Community... 265

Be A Better Parent App 266

Work Privately With Celia Kibler.................... 267

ABOUT THE AUTHOR

Celia Kibler 269

Do yourself a favor, do me a favor, heck, do your kids a favor and read this first!

I'm not calling this a Foreword or a "Note from the Author" or any of those titles that authors give that "real" first chapter of a book (you know, the one that doesn't say Chapter 1 and nobody reads) because if I do, **you won't read it.**

In short, I really want you to read it. You should read it. **YOU NEED TO READ IT.**
In reality, you have to start somewhere, so here is as good a place as any.

Honestly, why would I write it and put it in here, if I didn't expect anyone to read it?

So, smile, go forth, be intentional and start here at the first no-name chapter of this book.

Enjoy!

THE IMPORTANT STUFF
YOU REALLY NEED TO READ FIRST

Tod-dler / tådler /
1 (noun)
1.5 – 5 years. , an emotionally unstable pint-size dictator with the uncanny ability to know exactly how far to push you to utter insanity before reverting into the cutest, little, loveable creature you've ever laid eyes on

2 (noun):
a wild, out of control beast that lashes out, then laughs, then cries, then screams, then hugs, then laughs, then screams (it honestly can go on and on) and then runs crazy through the house… then trips, then falls, then drops into a deep sleep all in a matter of 20 minutes

This is the life of a toddler and you are their parent or caretaker, so this is your life too. These first five years are the most important years in your child's life, so make them great. Be intentional, be there for them, and learn all you can so they too can benefit. Laugh a lot. Love a lot. Have fun a lot.

Congratulations on starting with this book, because now you can really create a childhood that everyone can blossom from and no one has to recover from.

To say that you are about to take a long ride on this exhausting, emotional roller coaster is an understatement. To say it's a time that's filled with so many rewards is so very true.

The absolute truth is that this is the most precious human, and the wonder of watching them grow, day after day, is the best.

However, when this little human begins to drive you crazy, (and they will), it is easy to lose your mind and patience, all in a matter of minutes.

How is it that such a small person can bring out such a large reaction from us? How can they take a room from calm to absolute chaos? How can they make you wonder if you can survive another day?

Well, survive you will. You will go on to see this incredible creature grow up into a miraculous adult--that is, if you become intentional with your parenting and follow the advice in this book.
Every day, I hear parents say, "There are manuals for everything! Why isn't there a manual for kids?" Well, now there is!

The beauty of the information in this book is that it's not just for the toddler in your life, but it will help you work with your older kids. It will also come in handy as your child grows, year after year. In other words, there are sections in this book that your child will outgrow, (like potty-training), but the key information about intentional and proactive parenting, as well as the ways to empower your child, will last you, (and them), a lifetime.

Having a toddler can be loads of fun…if you can understand what makes them tick. Take the time to learn about this creature called "the Toddler" and start learning how you can get the upper hand on the energy, the emotions and the instability that is the nature of the beast. By going through the advice, techniques and strategies in this book, you will master your patience, and slowly realize how fun it is to create a childhood that you can all blossom from.

Let's discuss a few things that will help you on your journey.

THEIR BRAIN

Let's talk about brain power: theirs. The toddler brain is not anywhere near developed, in fact the human brain doesn't fully develop until about 23-25 years old. What??? Yup, it's true! So, if it takes about 25 years to mature, imagine how underdeveloped your toddler's brain is. After all, they have only been alive a very short amount of time.

This little brain is composed mostly of emotions and lots of them. This is why your child can move so easily from one emotion to the next, because, quite frankly, that's how they're wired.

What they are lacking is self-regulation, logic, rationale, compassion, understanding other people's needs and more. This is where you come in as their parent, coach, counselor, advisor and sometimes their partner, because, after all, you're in this together. You will take them through the processes to help them learn how to do things as they get older.

SEE THE WORLD THROUGH THEIR EYES

Never forget that you are not speaking to an adult. Expecting your child to respond to you as if they are an adult is ridiculous. Why? They're a toddler; they've only been alive for a few years and are working with an underdeveloped brain. They have very little real-life experience and see everything as new and exciting. Everything is something to touch, taste, feel, smell and learn about.

They are not doing things to make you mad, (although sometimes it seems this way), they are doing things because that's all they know how to do.

Let me give you an example. While enjoying a nice dinner out with my son, his wife and my grandkids, Mason, (at the time 1.5 years old), begins to get fidgety. Not in a bad way, more in a wiggly fun way. Dad looks at him and says:

"This is why we don't go out to dinner Mason, because you don't know how to act."

To which I replied, in a jovial sort of way:

"He's one and a half, he doesn't know how to act because he doesn't know how to act at all, anywhere."

Wiggling is one of the things toddlers and kids do. They wiggle, they jiggle, they laugh. You can't expect a duck not to quack; it's a duck.

In short, you need to understand the age of your child and the limitations they have. If you were three and you just saw a shiny new object, how would you react? You would get excited to learn more. That means touching, tasting and doing all those things that will gain you the knowledge that you seek. With that in mind, if you have a new item or something breakable sitting on a table, within your child's reach, I advise you to move it away, or it is liable to be handled by them.

Saying no 9,000 times a day doesn't make sense when you could actually be proactive: encourage your child to explore, to feel, to touch, to exercise their curiosity, but put away what you don't want touched. Yes, they will learn that some things can be played with and some cannot, but the more you make your home a safe, smart place for your child, the more you can say yes and create a more positive growing environment for everyone. The point is to see the world through your child's eyes. Understand their viewpoint and the age-appropriate behavior that they will present. When this realization is made, your guidance and direction of your child will be geared towards their ability to understand and you will all get along much better.

WHAT KIND OF PARENT ARE YOU?

Look deeply into how you were raised and think about what you liked about it. Now, think about what you didn't like. Realize that the voices in your head were placed there in your childhood. These voices will direct many of the ways you choose to parent.

Ask yourself these questions:

1. Do you hover over everything your child does? Are you constantly fearful that they will hurt themselves or get disappointed?

2. Do you feel like you need to control everything your child does? Do you feel like they must obey your every command? Are you putting rules and consequences in place just because you can and you want your child to know who's the boss?

3. Do you always want to be your child's friend? Do you feel like your child must always be happy and never cry?

4. Do you want your child to make all of their decisions with no responsibility or consequence?

5. Do you have no confidence in anything you do and your child(ren) just overwhelms you? Do you ask for everyone else's opinions? Do you just look at other parents with their kids and constantly doubt yourself? Is your house in complete chaos and you don't even want to come home half the time?

6. Do you feel like your parents were an excellent example for you? Do you think that maybe there could have been a better way than how you were brought up? Regardless of which one you identify with, are you determined to help your child(ren) stand on their own two feet? Are you willing to teach your child the skills they need to become a successful and confident adult? Are you determined to be there as their coach, confidante, teacher and guide, (while still allowing them to learn, make mistakes and know their self-worth), every step of the way?

Once you figure out what kind of parent you are, you can examine whether that is benefitting your child or compromising their growth and development. As you read through this book, you will find practical, easy to understand strategies and techniques that will help you increase your child's independence, find solutions and gain success, all the while keeping the synergy of the family in place.

Here are 23 key tips to remember as you travel on this journey with your toddler:
1. They are not adults.
2. They are full of emotions and not much else.
3. They are curious about everything (that's a sign of their intelligence and desire to learn).

4. They always want to please you, even if it doesn't seem that way.
5. They need to know you love them, regardless of how they are acting.
6. Don't take it personally.
7. Recognize their limitations.
8. Give simple instructions, one step at a time.
9. Give choices, but not more than two. Don't give the choice of NO if it is not an option.
10. If you make it fun, you will get it done.
11. 10-15 minutes of your uninterrupted time will mean the world to them.
12. Giving them a little control where you can will provide you with a lot of cooperation and listening throughout the day.
13. Chaos breeds more chaos, so calm down, keep your emotions in check and your child will start reacting calmly too.
14. Be the adult; don't expect them to be.
15. You are the boss of them, they are not the boss of you.
16. Read to them, a lot!
17. Allow your inner child to come out; put the fun back in your life.
18. Don't say it if you don't mean it.
19. Let them help whenever they can.
20. Give them their space; we all need a little alone time.
21. Observe them, tune in to them and discover and encourage their passions.
22. Love them, cuddle them, kiss them and tell them you love them.
23. Play with them, smile, laugh, run and have lots of fun together!

The more you understand your job in forming this miracle that you gave birth to, the more you will be creating one miraculous adult. The core values, growth mindset, confidence, self-worth, gratitude and happiness that you plant in them today will be the morals that they listen to tomorrow and all the days to follow. They will become the thoughts and voices in their head and instill positive behavior when approaching situations that require decisions, (good or bad). If you really recognize what your job is here, these five years will give them the tools they need to succeed in this game called life. Choose wisely parents; what you do, what you say and how you behave is the model that your child will build their foundation on. It will be what teaches them how to behave, how to react, how to listen to their heart and do what is best for them--not what someone is trying to persuade them to do.

Raising a toddler is a great responsibility because, in reality, you're actually raising an adult. They're amazing, fascinating little creatures, not to mention tons of fun--it's why I choose to hang out with them so much. They're awesome. They sparkle and love you unconditionally. They appreciate you in ways that even you don't. They look forward to every minute they get to be with you. They always want to please you because you are their world. They are always ready for more.

You bought this book and that shows me you have made a wise decision to become the parent your child deserves and the parent you know you can be. So, get started! Implement these tips and strategies. If you need help, reach out to me. Keep your child's light shining bright.

Now that you have decided to tackle this book and tame your toddler, I invite you to join, engage, ask questions and discover all of the supporting documents for this book beabetterparent.com. Feel free to join our public parenting group on www.facebook.com/groups/beabetterparent

Well, this is it. It's time to get rolling and learn about how you and your toddler can grow together and learn more about each other. Time to open your eyes to the truth about what you are dealing with. Time to be intentional and pro-active and the best parent you can be! YOU'VE GOT THIS!!! I believe in you. It's time to turn the page.

WELCOME TO RAISING HAPPY TODDLERS: HOW TO BUILD GREAT PARENTING SKILLS AND STOP YELLING AT YOUR KIDS.

The fun has just begun!

SECTION 1
CREATING FAMILY HARMONY

One

BECOMING A PRO-ACTIVE PARENT

So much of parenting is knowing your child--their behaviors and what can set them off. When you know their triggers, you can head them off at the pass. Becoming a proactive parent for your child allows difficult behaviors to occur less and less.

I hear parents getting upset at their child often because they're throwing a tantrum during a time when that child should be in bed, sleeping or eating. In my opinion, that tantrum becomes the parent's fault because you need to be able to schedule your day around keeping their basic triggers met.

SO HOW DO YOU BECOME PRO-ACTIVE INSTEAD OF REACTIVE?

Pro-active parents think before reacting. They plan ahead and envision what might be and prepare for it.

Let's first address the most common triggers for your child and understand that, if these are not addressed, your child will experience a meltdown or temper tantrum. These meltdowns are commonly caused by one of the following triggers:

HUNGER

Understand that, when your child is hungry, like any human, they will get irritable if they are not fed. That irritability will turn into tantrums, talking back, fighting, yelling, throwing, biting and a myriad of behaviors that most parents don't want to see.

What can you do? This is where being a proactive parent comes into play. Keep your child on a regular schedule of eating their meals and snacks. Don't plan activities that cause their meal schedule to go off track. If you need to take them somewhere and it's lunchtime, take a healthy snack for them to eat to satisfy their hunger.

If you are preparing dinner and your child is getting fussy, instead of yelling at them and telling them dinner is not ready yet, why not set out a tray of blueberries, grapes, carrot sticks…easy-to-snack-on foods that won't detract from their meal? This is a great time to set out vegetables which are often hard to get kids to eat. If they're really hungry, they'll eat them while they are waiting for the rest of their meal to be ready.

THIRST

Children dehydrate much faster than adults. When dehydration begins, the first thing affected in the human body is the brain. Because of this, the first symptoms you will notice are fussiness, whining and confusion. For this reason, I highly recommend that you have sippy cups of water placed in your home in strategic locations: the playroom, kitchen, and living room. Place the cups where your child can reach for them easily, avoiding the need to ask you for something to drink. Make sure there is fresh water daily in the cups. When your child gets thirsty, they'll just grab their sippy cup.

If your child is playing outside in high temperatures, be sure to always have lots of water and spray bottles filled with water available to keep their bodies cool.

SLEEP

Your child needs sleep, just like we all do, except he or she needs more. When they're sleepy, they get cranky.

Children between the ages of one and five need between 10 – 15 hours of sleep. All kids are different so this is a guideline and not the rule. The point is: at this age, your child should not be getting just 8 hours of sleep. It isn't enough.

I can't tell you how many times I have seen a parent with a toddler, out late at a restaurant, and get mad at their child because they're misbehaving. What did they expect? That child should be in bed.

Being tired is a huge trigger for negative behavior. Be smart, be intentional and give your child a solid sleep routine. See Chapter 39 for more details on sleep.

OVERSTIMULATION

Have you ever been in a busy store at Christmas? People are pushing, racing around, getting in your personal bubble. A toddler that is half the size of an average adult, when placed in a chaotic or crowded situation, will feel like you did in that store--totally overwhelmed and probably somewhat scared. This will trigger all kinds of reactions.

Again, be proactive. If you know you will be in a situation that will overwhelm your child, (and if it is an absolute must that they join you), be very aware of their environment so that you can support them when they need it. You may have to pick them up or sit on a couch with them. You can also take them to a separate room to relax and have some quiet time. You may even need to sit in the car with them for about 15-20 minutes to just talk, sing or play. Be sure that the other three triggers have been met before heading out to what could possibly be an overwhelming situation. Be aware of these things at family events and friend's parties.

Your Child's Party

A common event that overwhelms toddlers is their own birthday party. I have been conducting birthday parties for kids for over 30 years. Here is some advice that will allow your child's party to run as smoothly as possible without the risk of your child getting too overwhelmed:

During their own party or celebration.

1. Refrain from over-inviting to your child's party. A good rule of thumb is your child's age + two for the total number of invited guests. This is a guide not a rule, but I would stick as close to this number as possible.

2. Don't let this party run too long. The perfect length of time for a child's party is one to two hours.

3. Don't spend tons of money on a multitude of varied entertainment. This will overwhelm your child and your party guests. You run the risk of having all of your invited guests meltdown from exhaustion. Pick one entertainer and go with it.

4. Children love to run and play at a party. At this age, choose an entertainer that provides fun, active games and activities that are age appropriate and non-competitive. If you are having an active party like this, then play first, eat second.

5. If you choose to have entertainment that requires the kids to sit and watch, like a magician or storyteller, feed the kids first and then they will sit longer.

6. Concerning Costumed Characters, (can you say that real fast 10 times? Ha-ha). Know your child very well before booking someone in costume. Many costumed characters or clowns can scare small children. Think of it like this: Elmo is cute, red, fun and about 6 inches tall. Then you have a party and a 6 foot tall Elmo comes in. What??? Your child's reaction, "Holy cow, why is he so big?" It's scary and overwhelming to your child. It is not cute like the Elmo they know at all. I respectfully advise you to consider the size element when choosing a costumed character. If the character is already big, like Batman for example, then a big Batman coming to a party does not seem unusual to a child, although they still may be shy when reacting to the character.

7. Be proactive, do your homework, satisfy their triggers before, during and after their party and your child will have the best day of their life!

8. Being a proactive parent is a case of thinking things out before you do them. Understand the day ahead, stick as close to the routine and schedule as you can, and your child will reward you with positive, happy, cooperative behavior the majority of the time.

Two

PARENTING ON THE SAME PAGE

Before we go on with the details of actually parenting your toddler, let's discuss the two of you.

Regardless of whether you decided to have children or not, here you are with a child. Have you organized your thoughts on how your child(ren) should be raised?

In this chapter, I'm going to discuss the key areas of parenting a child. These are the areas where you and your partner will need to be on the same page. If these concepts are not agreed upon, you will run into problems as your child continues to grow. When parents don't agree, the child learns that they can play one parent against each other. Ultimately this will cause the breakdown of your relationship, not only as parents, but also as a couple.

Come up with a common vision of how you will operate as your child grows to become a productive adult member of society. Your child will begin to ask questions about things like school, church, etc., and you will want to have answers for them. Flying by the seat of your pants, although many people do it, is not in the best interest of your child, yourself or your family.

Let's begin with the 10 areas that I believe need to be addressed before you decide to start your family or as soon as possible after they are born. These 10 areas will make you intentional parents instead of parents that make no decisions, have no vision and just attack issues as they come up in a chaotic, reactive sort of way.

PARENTING METHODS

The first area that needs to be addressed is discussing what your parenting methods will be. During this discussion you may want to address how each of you were raised. What did you like about your childhood and what didn't you like? What are your individual beliefs on raising a child? Are you naturally calm, or does one, (or both), of you tend to yell a lot? Are you a nurturing person who says "I love you" a lot? Are you someone who likes to hug, kiss and show affection? Are you someone who is more reserved and has a hard time showing affection? Are you the type of parent who lets your child do as they please? Are you strict? Do you have a need to control whenever and wherever you can?

All of these questions need to be discussed as these behaviors will affect the way you parent your child. Talk about how you would like to raise your child(ren).

DISCIPLINE

Now think about how your parents disciplined you as a child. Will you do the same or do you plan on doing something different? Discipline is something that both parents need to agree on. Both parents should understand that what one parent says, the other one should support, regardless of which parent is disciplining. No parent should ever contradict the other in front of a child. If you disagree on something, discuss it out of earshot of your child(ren).

LANGUAGE

Do you both speak the same language? Is one language going to be primary over another? Does one parent curse more than another? Are you going to try to stop cursing in front of your child? Do you use your manners?

All of these questions are important to consider because the way you speak, will be the way your child speaks.

MONEY

A major frustration point in marriages, that can often lead to divorce, is the disagreement over money. Though this should be done before marriage, if you have a child and you haven't planned how you will handle your money, (so that you can afford the huge expenses of a child's lifestyle, like diapers, food, clothes, child care, medical fees, education, etc.), you need to start thinking about it and discussing it now. Will you share accounts and expenses? Will you have a joint savings account? Talk now about your spending habits and reach a happy compromise that works for both of you so it does not become an issue later.

RELIGION

Do you belong to the same religion? Do you practice the same way?

Do you both attend formal religious activities and worship? Is one of you more relaxed about it? If you belong to different religions, how will you raise your child? What will be consistent in your family? What ceremonies (or rituals) will be performed when a new child is born and as they grow? Talk it over until you are both in agreement.

EDUCATION

What is your educational plan for your child? Will education be a priority in your home? How will you school them as they grow? Homeschool, public or private? Are you planning on sending your child(ren) to college if that is what they need to fulfill their career paths?

SCREEN TIME

In this day and age, this is a prominent issue in the family. How will you create limitations and expectations of how screen time will enter into the family environment? Will there be time limits? Will there be a certain time of day when video gaming is allowed? How about TV and computer time? Will there be consequences if the family agreements of usage are not followed? Will computers be in a common area of your home so that you can easily see what sites your child is accessing? How do you plan to ensure their safety on the Internet? These are all good questions to ask yourself and to discuss with all parents and caregivers involved, before the need for these limitations arises.

NUTRITION

Often parents have different eating patterns or preferences. One parent could possibly like a lot of snacks and junk food, while the other parent eats a healthier diet. One parent may be vegan, while the other eats meat. One may need to follow a specific dietary program. It is important for you to discuss how this will affect the way you feed your child. If one finds it more important for your child to eat a certain way and the other does not agree, this will definitely create conflict between all family members.

HABITS/LIFESTYLE

This is a good time to take a long look at yourselves in the mirror and at each other. Your child will mimic what you do. If you know you have a habit that you're not happy with, and you prefer that your child not pick it up, now is the time to change it. Be each other's support and hold each other accountable for making changes. These habits can include smoking, drinking, spending habits, etc. Decide on what behaviors you want to teach your child and start adapting that lifestyle for yourself as soon as possible.

LOVE

All children need unconditional love, and by going through this exercise of making sure you are both on the same page, you will help your child feel safe and secure. They will know that their home is a place where they can find comfort and love at all times. Ask yourself: are you the type of person that mistrusts people initially? Are you quick to assume? Do you speak openly about your feelings or do you tend to hide everything? Do you kiss and hug in public and say "I love you" freely? Do you do this at home? Do you like to walk around naked in your home? How do you feel about doing this in front of your child? I encourage you to think things through with your partner so you both feel comfortable with each other's behavior.

In short, there are a lot of questions that you and your partner need to start discussing when starting a family. The areas I've listed here give you an excellent starting point. If there is something in your heart that you feel needs to be addressed, then it probably does. Don't wait until it builds up inside you and then you explode.

Being a pro-active parent is one of the best qualities you can possess. This chapter gives you some great questions to start asking yourself as you begin this journey. Always remember that children absolutely learn what they live

Children Learn What They Live

If children live with **CRITICISM**, they learn to **CONDEMN**.
If children live with **HOSTILITY**, they learn to **FIGHT**.
If children live with **FEAR**, they learn to be **APPREHENSIVE**.
If children live with **PITY**, they learn to feel **SORRY** for themselves.
If children live with **RIDICULE**, they learn to feel **SHY**.
If children live with **JEALOUSY**, they learn to feel **ENVY**.
If children live with **SHAME**, they learn to feel **GUILTY**.
If children live with **ENCOURAGEMENT**, they learn **CONFIDENCE**.
If children live with **TOLERANCE**, they learn **PATIENCE**.
If children live with **PRAISE**, they learn **APPRECIATION**.
If children live with **ACCEPTANCE**, they learn to **LOVE**.
If children live with **APPROVAL**, they learn to **LIKE** themselves.
If children live with **RECOGNITION**, they learn it is good to have a **GOAL**.
If children live with **SHARING**, they learn **GENEROSITY**.
If children live with **HONESTY**, they learn **TRUTHFULNESS**.
If children live with **FAIRNESS**, they learn **JUSTICE**.
If children live with **KINDNESS** and consideration, they learn **RESPECT**.
If children live with **SECURITY**, they learn to **HAVE FAITH** in themselves and in those about them.
If children live with **FRIENDLINESS**, they learn the world is a **NICE** place in which to live.

- by Dorothy Law Nolte

Three

BECOMING THEIR ROLE MODEL

Before reading this chapter, please read the poem by Dorothy Law Nolte on the previous page. Everything she wrote is absolutely true.

Many parents believe that children should do what they say, not what they do. This belief is the exact opposite of what actually happens through one's childhood. You can talk till you're blue in the face, but, if you are not doing what you are asking them to do, they will not do it either. If they do decide to do it, they will do it begrudgingly. Wouldn't it be easier if you would just model the behavior you want them to do? There would be less arguing, less discussion, less aggravation, because they will model the behavior of their strongest role models: YOU! Parents often ask me,

"How do I get my child to use their manners?"

The first question I ask them is: "Do you use your manners?"

The answer I always receive back: "Well, sometimes."

Let me tell it to you straight--if you want your child to use their manners, then you must use yours. Not just sometimes, but all the time. When they learn speech with manners attached, they learn that this is how we talk, and they proceed to speak as a well-mannered person.

The role models in a child's life, especially during the first five developmental years, have a huge influence over that child. Their parents, their caregivers, their relatives, their older siblings, their friends, all of those people who they see on a regular basis are the ones that mold them into the kind of person they are ultimately going to be. These are the people who give the child their character traits. This is where they build their habits, morals, spiritual base and they become the adult that they are going to be. Their primary caregivers, their parents, nannies, grandparents, whomever sees them on a daily basis, are the ones they model their behavior after.

Now, I ask you to stop and take a look in the mirror, so to speak. Write down 5-10 qualities about yourself that you would be proud to have your child inherit from you. Then, write down 5-10 qualities that you would not want your child to inherit. Start deciding how you are going to change so that your child doesn't pick up the same poor habits. If your habit is one that's hard to break, as most are, then be authentic with your child and let them help you break those habits. I had a friend who used to curse a lot and, after she had kids, she decided to start a "Dump the Habit Jar". She purchased a few rolls of quarters, and she told her children that every time she said an inappropriate word, they could take one quarter and drop it in the jar. At first, the jar was filling way too quickly, and she was astounded at how often they caught her using the words she was trying not to use.

After becoming more aware of just how often she did curse, she was able to start thinking before she spoke and eventually turned the habit around. The beauty is that her kids were able to take the responsibility for curbing her actions and help her create new healthier habits. In return, they learned what language was appropriate and what was not.

They also learned that Mom is human and that we are all allowed to make mistakes and try something again, if needed. It was a creative way to teach a lesson that everyone needed to learn. It required no yelling or screaming to get it done. Now it's your turn: what do you need to change for the sake of your child?

When parents realize that their actions will become their child's actions, they become more aware of their behavior.

LET'S HAVE SOME FUN WITH ALL OF THIS ROLE MODEL STUFF!

Here's a fun way to get a check on your behavior, as well as the way you speak to your child. First, watch the way they 'parent' their dolls. Do you see them doing things that you do with them? Do they say things that you say? Every child wants to be the parent, so I say, let them! Have a switch-around hour. You be the child and they will be your parent. A few pointers first: make sure if they tend to whine or throw tantrums, you mimic their behavior while you're acting as the child and see how they react to you. This can be a huge learning experience for all of you, but mostly it's a whole lot of fun and your child will love it!

Lastly, I want to mention that you should truly recognize how strong a role model you are to your child. When you see a child mimicking a negative behavior that they learned from you, there is no reason to yell at them. You taught them to do this. You can sit down with them and talk openly about how you made a mistake when you did it and you are sorry. Discuss ways that you can help each other remember that this is something you want to stop doing. When a family works together on a common goal, you teach teamwork, self-respect and confidence. Your child understands that you are all in this together, no one better than the other.

It is time to become the person that you want your child to be. Once you achieve this, you will find that your child is cooperating, listening, respectful and becoming a contributing member of the family.

Four

THE FAMILY MEETING: GETTING YOUR FAMILY ON THE SAME PAGE

Well, you are going to have kids and grow your family. You're not sure how it will all work, but everyone else does it, so how hard can it be?

Fast forward a few years and WOW, this is much harder than you thought. In fact, it's downright chaotic. You are a little, heck a lot, stressed! AHHHH!!!!

How will you ever get this group on the same page so that everyone knows who's coming and who's going?

Enter... THE FAMILY MEETING & THE FAMILY VISION!

What am I talking about? Does it sound a little too corporate? Well, you have this family, so you need organization and a plan. You need to know what is happening when and with whom. Basically, you need to know and keep track of a lot of stuff!!! Kind of like your job, right?

In order to create harmony in your family, everyone needs to be on the same page with each other. How do you this? You start conducting weekly FAMILY MEETINGS and sit back and watch as change happens.

Are you currently a parent in a blended family or are you considering starting one? I've been blessed with one for over 25 years and I can tell you that family meetings are essential in opening the lines of communication.

Are you ready to get started with this extremely important technique? Let's not waste any time. Remember that if your child is of toddler age, their contributions will be somewhat limited, but the importance of them attending the weekly meetings is no less valuable.

The first meeting you will have is the one where you create YOUR FAMILY'S VISION STATEMENT. There are no family goals unless you put them in place.

THE VISION STATEMENT

Here's the thing. We imagine our child being kind, cooperative, polite, fun, respectful, helpful and with so many more positive traits. THEN... they are born and start growing, and we're like... WHAT???? Where is my perfect child; where is the one that I imagined would be the envy of all other parents? Who is this child? Were they switched at birth?

No, no, no... that's your child, no switches, no aliens, no confusion. Just your child going about the business of being a toddler and wondering what they can touch, smell, disassemble, eat or jump off of next.

Enter the Vision Statement. This little power-packed paragraph is full of juicy life tidbits and goals that will put your family on the same page and create the belief and understanding that you are a family. You are all in this together.

DEFINITION: A Vision Statement, or as some may call it, a Mission Statement, is a short statement of your purpose, your goals, and methods of operation. This statement can also include your values and philosophies.

Are you seeing the bigger picture after reading the definition? Are you feeling why this might just be a great idea for your family? Well, take my word for it, it is.

Your vision statement will include the beliefs, core values and a simple statement or statements of how things will run in this home of yours for years to come.

Some food for thought. Think about and answer these questions...
Why did you decide to have a family?
What is your goal for your family?
What kind of person do you want your child(ren) to be?
How will this family run?
What will play an important role in your family?

Now list all the CORE VALUES that you want your child(ren) to possess as they grow. Ask your child(ren) to contribute their ideas. Even a toddler can contribute ways they should treat others, like being a good helper, being kind, being a good listener, using their manners, etc.

Here is a list of values to help you determine what you wish to focus on. Be sure to create your own list; this is just to get you started.

Kindness	Gratitude	Love	Compassion
Personal Growth	Perseverance	Politeness	Consistency
Honesty	Integrity	Fun	Happiness
Spirituality	Proactive	Family is Primary	Work Ethic
Rest & Relaxation	Harmony	Education	Respect
Being Intentional	Being helpful	Equality	Empowering
Excellence	Patience	Speaking Kindly	Sharing

If some of these agree with what you believe in, then go ahead and use them. If you have other things in mind, add them in. Now, narrow this list down to about 5-10 core values that you want to specifically include in your Vision Statement.

After you have these goals and values, create a list of expectations for the family as a whole and list specific items like attending Church or eating dinner together. Next, you want to formulate your statement out of these beliefs. Here is an example to guide you:

"In this family we love and respect each other. We offer to help when needed and work together to keep our home clean and tidy. We attend Church together each week and use kindness and manners when speaking to each other. We remain always grateful and fill our house with happiness and fun."

This should give you an idea of what a vision statement looks like and get you on the right track to creating your family's vision statement. At your first family meeting, your goal is to create this statement while allowing everyone in the family to contribute and then agree on it. Once the statement is written, everyone signs it and it is posted in a place of prominence where it can be seen daily. Your child can even help get creative with the design and decoration of the final product.

Now that you have your Vision Statement in place and everyone can see it, it's time to start planning for your weekly Family Meetings. Follow these guidelines. Feel free to add in your special personality to the way they operate, but make sure compliments always start and end your meeting.

Before you start, I'd just like to remind you of a few things.

HOW TO CONDUCT YOUR FAMILY MEETINGS

1. **Choose a consistent weekly time** for your Family Meetings so that everyone can attend as much as possible.

2. **Create a "TO BE DISCUSSED" Board** that you can post in an easy-to-see place (like a refrigerator). This is for anyone to write down situations that arise that they would like discussed at upcoming meetings. (You will find one to use if you go to "BeABetterParent.com").

3. **Find a comfortable location,** where everyone can be relaxed and attentive. Serve fun **snacks and drinks** to ease the mood.

4. **ALL ELECTRONICS & DISTRACTIONS OFF!**
No interruptions (except emergencies) at the meeting.

5. **Work on one main past issue and one new issue** at each meeting. This prevents overwhelming your child or causing the meeting to run too long.

6. **Meetings should last 15-20 minutes**, not any longer, (unless really necessary once in a while).

7. **Respect all opinions and listen** without criticism or judgement.

8. **Be flexible** with the discussion and be **willing** to **put your child's ideas into action** whenever possible. This is a family meeting. This is where you will begin creating the atmosphere that you are all in this together. You are building respect for each other and each other's opinions. You want your child to feel perfectly comfortable speaking up and offering their own ideas into the discussion.

9. **Always have a Meeting AGENDA** in place for each meeting.

FAMILY MEETING AGENDA

A. Compliments, (served up by each parent to each child). I don't care if the past week was a disaster, think of one thing that you can compliment your child on).

B. REVIEW what went on in the past week.
  1. What was the issue?
  2. Was the issue resolved successfully?
  3. Do you need to brainstorm another solution?
     (HEADS UP: Put in place your child's solutions as often as you can; this will go a long way towards building respect and confidence in each other.)
  4. If needed, choose a new solution to try this week.
  5. Review how the new solution worked at next week's meeting

C. NEW BUSINESS: DISCUSS a new issue from the "To Be Discussed" Board. Discuss in the same manner.

1. What was the issue?
2. Was the issue resolved successfully or what happened that caused it to be written on the board?
3. Do you need to brainstorm another solution? (Reminder: It's great to put in place your child's solution to the problem as much as you can)
4. If needed, choose a new solution to try this week.
5. Review how the new solution worked at next week's meeting.

D. REVIEW this week's schedule… what's on the schedule, who's driving, what conflicts, special events, etc.

E. Have each person talk about something wonderful that someone in the family did for them.

F. Each person talks about something they are grateful for.

G. Let everyone know when the next meeting is (if it is being held at a different time)

H. Meeting adjourned.

CONGRATULATIONS!! You're on your way to really building a family that respects each other, works together and has an all-in attitude that will benefit everyone.

These meetings will become part of your family life. Have fun at your meetings and don't let them go too long. Stick to your agenda, treat everyone with respect, listen carefully and I promise you, your child will look forward to and love attending every single one.

Five

WORKING PARENTS: FINDING BALANCE

You have kids, you have work, you have the house…could you possibly fit anything else into your 24-hour day? Oh yeah, you need to sleep and eat. It's clearly not just a job, it's an adventure and one that can stress out even the calmest human. So, how can you find balance? How can you find your calm and patience? How can you find just 15 minutes to relax and breathe? On top of it all, you find yourself feeling guilty for…oh…everything!

So, where do I begin to help you regain your identity and still have fun with your child and with your hectic life?

Working parents often feel guilty that they have to go to work or, if they work in the home, that they are not with their kids. So, parents, I am here to tell you that you do not have to feel guilty any longer.

After all, what are you teaching your child by being a working parent?

1. You are teaching your child a good work ethic by demonstrating consistency and being proud of a job well done. Work Ethic is something that all parents need to be instilling in their kids. Otherwise, children become entitled adults that are just going through the motions of work and taking zero pride in what they are doing and how they are doing it.

2. What can you do to help?
Talk about your day with your child. Talk to them about problems that came up throughout the day and ask them how they would have handled certain situations. Discuss what you did to resolve the problem and how it worked out for you. Do you think you will need to try a different process or did your way of approaching the issue work? Be authentic with your child, even if you feel you have made a mistake and are brainstorming different processes. This is directly teaching them that we all should not fear mistakes but welcome them as part of the learning and growing process.

Let's talk about spending time with your child.

You need to make it count! You may not have as much time to spend with your child daily, but the time you do spend with them needs to be quality time. Time that is just you and them doing something fun together, like games, puzzles, crafts, art, music, dancing, having a picnic, etc. The time you spend with your child is what will form their memories of their childhood. Instead of thinking, "My parents were always working," they will remember the playtime, the laughter, the goofiness and the general warmth of sharing the love and delight that you find in each other.

What can you do to help make your time together go smoother and happier?

1. Put down the distractions! Put your cell phone away, tablets, TV. Whatever will take away from your one-on-one time with your child, put it away. All of that can wait; your child will never be this age again. Every day they grow older and the special stages and events that you miss will not return.

2. Household chores can wait. Although household chores should be shared by everyone in the house, (even your child), I recommend that after a long day of work, you make the best of this time by enjoying a little rest, relaxation and fun with your child! We will discuss ways to make chores fun for everyone in Chapter 29.

3. Take a lesson from your dog. Even if you don't have a dog, most of us know that when a dog sees its owner, even after being apart for just a half hour, the excitement is out of control. The tail is wagging, the tongue is swinging, the joyful howling begins. They can barely control themselves. As a parent, you should be equally as excited to see your child when you come home from work or when they come home from school or daycare. If you get home first, get up, greet them at the door and talk about how their day went. Your child should know that they are the most important thing in your life at that moment and that you missed them as much as they missed you.

Even if you've had a bad day, (and we often do), hide it for the moment and get excited about seeing your child. After you have happily welcomed each other, then you can say, "I'm going to change and then we can spend some special time with each other."

The idea is for those few moments when you see each other for the first time, you need to greet them with all the excitement you can muster.

4. Always say "Goodbye". Often parents decide to avoid the drama of separation by not saying goodbye. This is exactly the opposite of what you should be doing. One of toddlers' biggest fears is that their parents are leaving and never coming back. When you leave and do not say goodbye, it only reinforces this fear. They have no idea where you have gone and when, or if, you are coming back. Whereas, if you say goodbye and tell them when you will be back, whether they completely understand or not, when you return each day, it will begin to alleviate their fears and increase their comfort levels when it's time to separate. This does not mean that they will not have any anxiety from you leaving, but the emotional expressions will get better and eventually come to an end**.**

5. If you have a workplace in the home, whether you work either part-time or full-time, try to have an area that allows you to close the door to avoid constant distractions. Consider it as, what I like to call, the 'STOP LIGHT' approach for your office door (if you only have a room divider this can also easily work for that). The idea is to use the colors red, yellow and green to signal when you are available for an interruption by your child. Cut large circles out of each color and use Velcro so that the circles can be easily attached and removed from the door or divider.

RED: When the RED CIRCLE is on the door, that means NO INTERRUPTIONS. Simply explain to your child that RED means that you are in the middle of something important and cannot talk to them until you are done. That means no knocking or interruptions of any kind.

YELLOW: When the YELLOW CIRCLE is showing, that means that you may be able to be interrupted, given that they knock first. You will address them and let them know if this is a good time to talk.

GREEN: When the GREEN CIRCLE is showing, even if the door is still closed, your child is welcome to come in and interrupt you with whatever they need.

Remember to discuss this new method of operation at your Family Meeting (see Chapter 4) and explain how it works. Allow your child to offer their ideas and opinions as well.

6. Find a good caregiver in your absence, whether it's in or out of the home.
-   a. The caregiver(s) should be someone who loves being around children and delights in their behavior and growth. This will help you feel confident that they will love your child almost as much as you.

-   b. Discipline techniques should align with what you believe in and you should be open to discussing how they handle situations that require discipline.

-   c. The environment (home or business) should be maintained and completely safe for a child. Materials that are hazardous or harmful should be locked up. There should be proper supervision at all times. The place should be clean and consistently sanitized and made free of germs as much as possible.

d. Staff should be washing their hands and have a safety routine in place for handling bodily fluids like vomit, blood and feces.

e. You should be aware of the daily schedule and ensure that there is plenty of active time for your child to play, interact with other kids, allow for physical and cognitive development, and enjoy an overall calm environment that is nurturing, filled with communication and fun. Screen time should be at a minimum (if any at all), with reading, games and creative play time, being the focus for the majority of their day.

f. Feel free to ask to observe a day in their home or building before making your decision to leave your child there. Also ask for references so that you can talk to other parents that have children in the facility.

g. The facility should provide daily written reports to you of your child's progress, including food that was consumed, as well as discipline, social and work behaviors.

h. In short, don't just settle for the first place you find. Caregivers often spend more time with your child than you if you are a full-time working parent. If you want them raised with your beliefs, then take the time to find a caretaker that has your wishes and your child's needs at heart.

The truth is that some of us, in fact most of us, have to work. You can work on creating calm and structure in your home or you can have complete chaos, causing everyone stress. Work can be stressful enough, so be intentional with the way your family works together and you can come home to relax. Yes, even with kids.

Six

SIBLINGS: CALMING THE CHAOS, BREAKING THE BATTLES, CREATING COMMUNITY

So, you have these children and you're thinking "All they do is fight." First of all, is that really true? Take some time to start noticing the positive things that they do together. The hugs, helping each other, the chats, the laughter. It's easy to only see the disagreements, arguments, and battles. But try to really start tuning into your child. Start seeing the love between them and all the good that they do. Start complimenting their cooperative ways, calm play, and kindness towards each other. That alone will go a long way to maintaining more peace in your household.

If you had siblings growing up, reflect for a moment on your daily grind. What do you remember about it? Was it mostly fighting? Was it the private jokes you had between each other? Did you build forts and play as a team? Did you feel bullied in your own home by your older siblings? All of this reflection will help you deal better with your children and their behavior. Remembering your life when you were growing up will help you to understand why you react the way you do to your children, when they start behaving in a certain way. Their behavior is usually triggering a past emotion for you.

Let's use all of these events in your past and start becoming proactive so you can be calmer and more constructive to your children in the present and future.

Like I said at the start of this chapter, start focusing on the positive. What do your children do right? What works for them? What allows them to work with each other instead of against each other?

Now answer these questions. Are you favoring one child over the other? Are you comparing one child to the other? Do you always defend or take the side of the same child when they break into an argument? I beg you to be honest with yourself. If the answer is yes to any of these questions, your behavior is igniting their behavior. You are creating jealousy and an overactive need for attention from your children. These behaviors usually result in increased arguments, fights and turmoil.

Now that you have recognized your own behaviors and how it may be contributing to the behavior of your children, let's talk about all the good that results from having a sibling before we address how to handle the occasional dispute.

Take some time to have a family meeting and ask everyone, including yourself, to say 2 or 3 things that they like about each person in the family. This not only gives everyone a chance to focus on the good that someone does, but it also shines a light on the joy that we bring others when we behave kindly and compassionately. You will begin to see the faces of your children light up as they discover that the little things they do, are being noticed and really seem to matter. Watch them light up when they hear you, their parents, recognize their efforts. This goes a long way towards making everyone feel that they are valued, respected and happy about being a part of this family. They don't just start looking at each other differently but they begin to look at themselves differently and recognize that kindness, caring and empathy for others really do make a difference.

Before we get into resolving sibling spats, let's get into the benefits of having a sibling.

First and foremost, you have a built-in buddy, a companion; someone who knows all that there is to know about you and has shared your life from the beginning, (or almost the beginning). Your sibling will have compassion for you, having been by your side for the challenges and the successes.

Older siblings give younger siblings someone to look up to and emulate that's not their parents. Someone who they trust and may find easier to talk to. An older sibling is a family member who will share life with them, hopefully long after their parents are gone. However, we all know that it doesn't always work out this way. You may even have a sibling, as you're reading this, who you don't get along with at all and you never speak to. Sadly, there are no guarantees in life. Life has its ups and downs, but, while your children are little, and with you becoming an intentional parent, you have a much better chance of creating a sibling relationship that will last a lifetime.

There are many life skills that children learn from a sibling. One, as you might have guessed, is conflict resolution. When siblings are allowed to resolve their simple problems without adult interference, it helps them learn skills that they can use as adults to resolve future issues that arise. However, even when adults interfere, as arguments and conflicts between children can get too heated to just let them work it out, they also learn more advanced techniques of solving a dispute. Children learn how teamwork can make a lot of things work. When working together cooperatively, they may reach a better result than if they had just tried to complete the task on their own.

As I mentioned before, siblings learn empathy and how to be compassionate to others. An older sibling very often will stand up for their younger sibling when called to do so. This gives the younger sibling the confidence that someone always has their back and that provides additional security and comfort beyond their parents. A sibling is a peer, friend, mentor, advisor, and teacher.

A sibling is a peer, friend, mentor, advisor, and teacher.

Let me share an example with you from when my children were growing up. When my son Kyle came home from the first day of 5th grade, his homework assignment in math was concerning Pi, something I was never very good at. I shared with him, while we laughed, that I'm pretty sure that is where my math education ended when I was in high school. So, from that point on, when Kyle had issues with learning math, (although he shortly became quite good at math), he would consult with his older sister for advice and explanations. Having Lauren there was so helpful as she had recently been through a lot of what he was learning and found it easier to explain things to him, rather than me. That would not have been available to him, had he not had an older sibling.

Now I know what you're thinking, this sounds so simple in concept, however, "If I have to hear those kids fighting one more time, I'm going to lose my mind!" So, let's explore what you can do to handle the disagreements that do and will arise between siblings.

WHEN SIBLINGS FIGHT

First off, I want you to start becoming aware of the level of conflict occurring. As we know, there can be small disagreements and really big ones. Therefore, you need to be aware of what exactly is going on, before you jump right in and intervene.

Very often as parents, when we hear one of our children start to yell or another one start to cry, our immediate impulse is to end the noise and solve the problem. However, this is not your wisest move.

Here are the three levels of a sibling (or friend) argument that you need to be aware of before reacting and interfering:

1. Small minor disagreements. YOU: Stay out of it. Ex: Brother has a car, sibling wants the car; they yell, they cry and then they move on and sibling that wanted the car gets a different car. Problem solved, no pain, lots of gain; they learned to resolve the problem all by themselves, adding to their own experience with conflict resolution.

2. Escalating disagreements. YOU: Monitor the activity and intervene if necessary. Ex: Brother has a car, sibling wants the car; they yell, they cry, they continue to scream louder and louder. Other sibling that wants car runs to you to solve the problem. You can suggest how they can play together without an argument (find another car to play with) and stay close by as they resolve the problem and be available to offer further assistance if needed. At this point, hopefully they have proceeded with the option you offered or even better, they came up with a solution all on their own.

3. Violence has ensued. YOU: BREAK IT UP. Do not allow your kids to start hitting, throwing items at each other, biting or bullying of any kind. If the conflict has escalated to this level, you need to break it up by separating the two of them into different areas. Once they have calmed down (and once you have calmed down), then you can all talk about what happened, what they could have done to solve the problem, and how you can work to prevent it from happening again. At this point, you can also discuss a consequence that you can all agree on, if it does happen again. This consequence will help them to think twice before letting a dispute escalate to this level of violence.

Now here are some additional tips that I want you as a parent or caregiver to remember, that will encourage your children to relate to each other in a more positive way.

1. DON'T ASSUME: Don't assume you know who is at fault. Listen to the whole story from all parties before making a judgment. If you need to, talk to each participant privately, so that you are sure you are getting all the facts, and no one is feeling intimidated.

2. DON'T COMPARE YOUR KIDS in any way, at any time, in front of them. When you do, you automatically cause one child to feel superior to the other. Do not label them or call them names. Don't say things like: "Oh, she's the lazy one" or "He's the good one." That creates automatic conflict and resentment toward each other and they will start having low-self-esteem when given negative titles. Consequently, they may also feel like they're better than everyone else when given a title that suggests they are superior in some way to their siblings.

3. GIVE OLDER CHILDREN THEIR SPACE. Don't constantly put an older child in charge of a younger sibling or have the younger sibling accompany the older one to social situations. There is no reason for both of them to attend an event that is intended for only one. If you are concerned that the younger one may feel left out, then speak to them about how they can't always go with their sibling and take this as a great opportunity to spend some special one-on-one time with the younger one. We all need our own space and time, so give it to them. Don't always throw them together. A lot of conflict can be resolved by allowing for a little individual peace and quiet.

4. "WELL, YOU'RE OLDER AND YOU SHOULD KNOW BETTER." This is such a common thing for a parent to say to the older child; however, you need to remember that they are still children and are still learning about self-regulation and emotions. They are NOT their sibling's parent, nor should they be expected to act like they are. If you think they should know better about a way they reacted to a situation, then instead of just slamming them for their behavior, talk about alternate ways that they could have reacted when presented with the same problem again. This will continue to teach them to think before reacting and help them to build their ability to self-regulate. Remember, the human brain does not fully develop until the age of 25. It is our job as parents to guide them into making well thought-out decisions.

5. DISTRACTIONS WORK. Sometimes all your children need is a little distraction. Maybe they have simply been with each other too long and they need a break. Put on some music, dance, play with balloons, bring out a board game that you can all play, go outside and get some fresh air. Think of how you can change the scenery for them, and it will give them a way to turn off what is fast becoming a negative situation.

6. SHARE ONE-ON-ONE TIME WITH EACH CHILD. Be ure to set up special times where you and one of your children do something special together, without any of their siblings. Read books, take a walk or play a game. The idea is to be involved and present with each of your children, one at a time, so you can focus solely on them, confirming in their mind that they are still very special to you. This is especially important if there is a new baby in the house. My kids are all in the 30s and we still enjoy one-on-one time with each other. It honestly never gets old.

7. GET INVOLVED. Bring yourself to their level of fun and play WITH them, don't just sit nearby and watch. Often sibling spats are over trying to get your attention. When you are able to give them your full attention, even if it's just for 10 or 15 minutes, it will mean the world to them and they will move on to playing with each other after you have left, with little or no conflict.

8. TAKE NOTICE. When your children are getting along well or doing a behavior you would like them to continue, point it out to them, let them know you noticed, and compliment them. Children ultimately want to please their parents and, when they discover they are pleasing you, the behavior that made you happy is the one they'll want to repeat.

9. BE PRO-ACTIVE. to discuss issues that have come up over the past week and start brainstorming how you can resolve tension in the future. Be authentic with your children and start telling them how you resolved conflicts that came up at work or how you and your siblings diffused arguments when you were a child. These family meetings will create a team mentality and the realization that we all need to be working together, not against each other.

10. RECOGNIZE BOUNDARIES. We all have personal boundaries and limits on our personalities and emotions. Allow your children time and space to themselves and don't continually push them on each other. Allow for each child's independence, while respecting their need to be an individual. This will go a long way in creating a positive relationship when it comes to their time spent together.

Seven

YOUR GROWING FAMILY: GETTING YOUR TODDLER READY FOR A NEW BABY

Let's imagine for a minute that you are the center of your parent's world. You are their baby. They love you and you love them. They are everything. When Mommy or Daddy hold you, you are secure, safe and feel totally loved. It's the happiest place on earth for you.

Then… Mommy leaves. She's not there for a while and you are worried. You're scared; you don't know what to expect. But wait, Mommy is here, "Yay!!! She's home!". You go running up to her and… what's this? What is Mommy holding? A baby!!!! Another baby, not you! A cute little thing and they tell you this is your brother or sister. They say, "You will love your new baby!" "You will have so much fun with this baby!" "This is YOUR baby."

AAAAHHHH!!!

What happened to me? I AM the baby!! I AM your baby!! Where did this baby come from? Why is it here? Did I ask for a baby? Can we take it back? Ok, maybe it can stay for a little bit and maybe I will tolerate it, but then, return it! Give it to someone else. We are all filled up here. We have a baby and that baby is ME!!!!!

Funny as this scenario is, it is exactly what is going through your child's head, whether you would like to believe it or not. They are feeling like they have been replaced and they are worried, scared and stressed, because they don't know what to expect or what will happen next. Their security, their happy life, everything they have known so far is thrown into total chaos, because their loving parents now have ANOTHER BABY!!!

Even with preparation, many of these thoughts will still run through your child's head when the reality of another child is brought into the home. You owe it to your child to prepare them. The transition will go much easier and life for all of you will be more peaceful (at least as peaceful as it can be considering there is a new baby in the house).

PREPARING YOUR LITTLE ONE IS A MUST!

Let's talk about how you can prepare your child for the arrival of a new sibling. First of all, remember that toddlers do not have awareness of time. Do not tell your toddler that they are getting a new baby just after you get pregnant. I know you're excited to share the news, but they will then bug you for the next 8 months about when this sibling is coming to their house. Instead, wait until your belly really gets big enough for them to notice a true difference in your body and then you can start talking to them about it.

When you introduce the concept of the arrival of a sibling, first talk about when they were a baby. Share pictures, movies, memories and let them see what happened when they came home.

Now, this is where most parents stop with their idea of preparing their toddler for a new baby. I implore you to not stop here. You need to realize that what will really throw your child for a loop, is not only their lack of knowledge of what a new baby means to their world, but their frustration and jealousy that will be created by a baby's need to be attended to regardless of what is going on in the household and specifically what is going on with them.

Here is how you will really prepare your child for life with an infant - and start doing this about two months before their sibling's arrival. First, get them a doll, yes, even if they are a boy. This doll will represent their new sibling. Start roleplaying real life scenarios with the doll. Have your toddler help with jobs like diapering, feeding and playing. Sit down to play a game with your toddler and put the baby to sleep in a toy crib or on blankets and then pretend it woke up crying and interrupted the game you were playing. Make a point to say:

"The baby is awake, we need to go get him, (or her). After we help the baby, we can go back to playing."

Then let them help you with tending to the baby. Do this same thing at mealtimes, getting ready for school and in any situation where the real baby may interrupt an activity that is already in progress. This will help them to adjust to infant interruptions way before the baby is born.
Start reading books about being a big brother or sister. Tell stories about when you became a big sister or brother, (if you did).

Discuss what jobs they think they can help you with when the baby comes home and role play that with the doll. If they want to get diapers for you, let them. If they want to help with bottles, bibs or blankets, let them. Maybe they want to help entertain the baby with a rattle or by singing. There are all kinds of ways a toddler can contribute.

Continue to do this up to the time the baby is expected. When the day comes for you to give birth, prepare them for that too. After all, you will be away, and they will be confused and stressed. Talk to them about where you are going, what will be happening, and how long you expect to be away. Keep details age-appropriate. Get them excited about things they can do to prepare the house while you're away. Have family and friends plan outings for them, so they have special time as well. Toddlers are all about themselves and your job is to get them excited about welcoming another child into their world.

When the baby comes home, talk to your toddler about all the things you were able to do with their doll. Remind them that they can still be helpful with their new sibling. Go over the need to be delicate when handling the baby and review all the ways that they can help with their sibling's care. Remind family and friends who bring over presents for the baby to please bring a small little gift for the big brother or sister. If you feel awkward with that, you may just want to go to the dollar store and buy some books, crafts items, bubbles and little gifts that you wrap before the baby gets home. Make sure that the entire household doesn't become totally centered around the new baby and your toddler is pushed aside and forgotten. They will feel a little like that anyway, due to the excitement that naturally comes with a new baby.

Share with your toddler the fun they will have as they watch their baby brother or sister grow. One day, they will be buddies and be able to play together, laugh and have fun, but not right away, since new babies need all of our help until they get bigger.

Talk about how they can be a great teacher. Help them name all the cool things they already know because they're so big and get them excited about teaching those things to the baby.

Keep in mind, a new baby will always create a bit of jealousy in the older sibling. It may not show its face right away, but it will show up eventually. It's only natural. Your toddler may revert to some "baby" activities that you thought they were done with like sucking their thumb, wetting the bed or crying more. All of this is natural as they adjust to competing for your time.

Rest assured, this will work itself out and the benefits of having a sibling will far outweigh the adjustment period. However, the more you prepare your toddler for the new arrival, the easier the adjustment will go.

Eight

SPECIAL KIDS, SPECIAL LOVE

You dream about what your child will be like as you go through your pregnancy, we all do. You imagine the perfect child with ten fingers, ten toes, a strong body and a strong mind. You imagine a happy and loving child.

Then the day arrives when you get to meet your little angel and this one comes out just a little bit different; not in a bad way, but in a very special way. You might have known things were a little different prior to birth, but sometimes, even with all of today's technology, some things are still a surprise. Your mind is spinning. Your heart is exploding, and your brain is shooting out every emotion you can imagine: excitement, curiosity, anxiety, nervousness, confusion, happiness, sadness, but most of all, lots of love. This one's yours, this little bundle of joy that you finally get to hold, kiss and love.

Your miracle is born, but there are some issues that will have to be addressed. Are they lifelong issues? Are they temporary issues? The journey begins...

Here is a little guidance that I have learned over my 35 plus years of working and teaching within the wonderful world of children with challenges. I will also share my thoughts of having to wear a full body brace from 8th grade to 12th grade due to scoliosis and how those five years impacted my life and my beliefs for the better. I will also talk about how I felt and viewed the world of people who looked at me as different. In addition, you will notice that a lot of the advice I offer in this chapter will relate to any of your children, but this one especially.

First off, smiles can and should happen. Your child just wants to be like everyone else. They want to laugh, play, be silly, be angry, be smart, be capable and be whatever they dream they can be. In other words, they just want to be a regular kid.

Organization and routines will be your best friend.

Keep papers, schedules and your household orderly. Chaos breeds chaos, and a messy environment creates chaos in our minds, attitudes and behaviors. Depending on the amount of doctor and therapist appointments your child will be required to have on a regular basis, this alone can make a daily schedule very chaotic. Coming home to an orderly house, where papers are easily found and you're not tripping over things everywhere you walk, will help calm anxiety and stress. This doesn't mean you need to constantly focus on your home being spotless and tidy. Actually, if your house needs cleaning and straightening and your child also requires attention, I encourage you to opt for hanging out with your child and leave the cleaning for later. Encouraging your child to be a part of the organization and order of the house is not just a suggestion, it should be viewed as the responsibility of all members of the family. Refer to Chapter 29 concerning chores and start your child working on their own space and sharing the responsibility of family areas in your home. Everyone, regardless of their age, (toddler on up), can and should contribute something to the order of your home. Depending on abilities, responsibilities should be tailored appropriately.

If you have more than one child, be sure to treat all of your children normally.

Yes, some of your children may require very special attention, depending on their needs; however, if your special child has siblings, be sure to spend intimate time with them as well. You don't want your other children to become jealous and resentful because your full attention is always on their sibling. This will happen if they are always in the background of your attention and never the foreground. Yes, your child who requires extra attention must have what they need when it is needed, but that child's sibling needs it too, and they need to know that you love them just as much. Make sure they feel your love for them even though they don't have any urgent medical needs themselves. Lack of attention is why the other children in the family start acting out or mimicking the needs of their sibling. In their mind, if they had some challenges too, you would pay more attention to them. So, be sure to offer all of your children the much-needed personal attention that they require. Read to them, play with them, take each of them to special places on their own for one-on-one time with each parent. This is important for all kids in your family, regardless if your family includes children with challenges or not.

Children need to be reminded that, on their own, they are extremely important to you and unconditionally loved. Consistent one-on-one time reinforces those feelings, even if it's just for 10-15 minutes here and there.

Know that you're not alone.

Parenting is never easy and, when you add in medical challenges, it makes it that much more difficult. Don't feel guilty, don't feel isolated; feel motivated. Start meeting new people, making new friends, reaching out to support groups online and in your community. The more open you are to meeting new friends, the more they will react with encouragement and support. Join classes that involve children and parents for active playtime. Consider mainstreaming your child to start building bridges of communication and familiarity. This will also help participants feel comfortable in what might be an uncomfortable situation for many.

Let me give you a personal example. When I wore my body brace all day and would go into stores, often, it was not other children who acted strangely towards me or stared continuously; it was the adults. They're the ones that would make me feel uncomfortable. When I think back on those five years, I mostly remember the ignorance of adults with their comments and stares. Sure, I have some memories of a few kids who were not so nice, but overall, it was the adults who caused my anxiety and discomfort on a weekly basis. I highly recommend that, if you're able to, you mainstream your child into a class that is open to all, helping to build bridges of understanding for everyone.

Here's an example of the success of mainstreaming: In my fitness classes for toddlers, one little girl had a walker and braces on her legs. Her mom asked if they could join my class, (which is quite active), and I encouraged their participation. Once the class began and the other toddlers in the class noticed her walker, each child wanted to know why they didn't get one. They loved it! The little girl got stronger and stronger in the class and was often walking and playing without the use of her walker, allowing other kids to try the walker too. It was a great experience for everyone!

We make mistakes. As parents, we must always remember: we are all human. Although we have the best intentions, we may not always be right. Accept that, learn from your mistakes and move on. If you need to try it again, then do so. Honestly, I don't even like to use the word "mistakes" because it has a negative connotation. I would rather call them "speed bumps" along the way of this crazy road we call life. If you hit a speed bump, learn from what happened, rethink the path and keep going. Never fault yourself for trying something new because you thought it may result in something you thought would work and it just didn't pan out. Every small step in the right direction should be celebrated, complimented and encouraged, regardless of who took that step, you or your child.

Make life fun for all of you. Play, laugh and smile when you're at home. Sign up for programs that encourage you and your child to participate together in movement activities, craft, art, outdoors and result in lots of happiness.

Lastly, I want to advise you to go with your heart. You know your child better than anyone else. I am sure, by now, you have learned almost all that there is to know about what your child faces. So, trust in your heart and don't listen to other uninvited opinions. Stay on track with your beliefs and reach out to people you trust with your questions. Always let your child know how much you love them. The two of you are walking this road together; get the help you need for you and your child and continue to put one foot in front of the other.

Nine

PATIENCE: TAMING THE STORM

When asking a group of parents what is the one thing they feel they need to improve upon when parenting their child, the overwhelming response is "patience".

I felt that this chapter for this book was not only necessary, it was absolutely mandatory. Gaining more patience is a matter of putting in place all of the tips I give you in this book, especially within the first section that deals with family harmony. The more harmony you have in your family, the less chaos; the less chaos you have, the less stress; the less stress, the more calm you have; the more calm, the more you can relax and enjoy family life. Get your schedules and routines in place, learn to smile, use your manners when you speak and add in more gratitude every day.

The number one thing to remember is that we all need a good night's sleep. Without properly resting the body, a person, big or small, is irritable. When you, as a parent, experience a lack of sleep, you become less patient with everyday issues. Refer to Chapter 38 on sleep to discover ways that everyone in your family can sleep more soundly and restfully.

Eating healthy, drinking lots of water, exercising and feeling physically well and energetic will also increase your patience.

Here's a few tips for when you lose your patience, whether it is at home, work, meetings or wherever.

1. Take three. Simply put, before reacting to a negative situation that you would normally lose patience with, take a three minute time out to relax yourself, think clearly and come up with your best response for whatever has elevated your nerves. You can then approach the situation calmly and productively and the people that you are directing your response to will remain calm as well.

2. Don't take it out on your child. If something caused you to be aggravated during your day and you come home to your child, be sure to greet them with love and feel free to explain to them that you need to go relax from a stressful day. Let them know that you need to rest a little and then you will come to play with them. If you unintentionally respond to your child based on the mood you are in from your day, apologize and tell them why you reacted like that. Then, collect yourself and play with them or approach the situation in a more sensible, kind way.

3. Destress. Turn off the noise. If the TV is on, video games are on, if there is a lot of background noise, turn it all off and have about 10-15 minutes of silent time for everyone. During this time, your child can read, you can relax or meditate, and you can start calming the stress for everyone in your home. Unclutter your house. Clutter is environmental stress and will cause a person more stress just from being in a cluttered room. Make a family project to clean up one room at a time until the whole house is done. It's a great project for when your child is out of school. Even your toddler can help clean up (see Chapter 29 on chores). The more you ask them to help, the better they will be at picking up stuff.

4. Have fun & start laughing! Start seeing the entertainment value of your child. I'm telling you, they're pretty darn funny if you just sit and watch. Laughter really is the best medicine; it relieves stress and it calms the nerves.

> *"Laughter is an instant vacation!"*
> ~ Milton Berle

Fake it if you have to. As a Laughter Yoga Leader, I will tell you that is the basis of laughter yoga. You get all the health benefits by doing various exercises that are accomplished through fake laughter. Did you know that fake laughter is just as stimulating to the brain, brings on the same hormones and the same emotional response as real laughter? Did you know that when you laugh, you not only relieve your stress, but it will relax your muscles for up to 45 minutes after you have had that good laugh? Laughter has so many healthy benefits to the human body aside from the fact that it is just simply fun. Laughter burns calories! What??? Yes! Are you looking to lose weight? Want to fit in a little exercise into your otherwise busy day? Start laughing more! Just 10 to 15 minutes of laughter can burn approximately 40 calories. Imagine the benefits of a whole afternoon of fun! Here's the truth, nothing can break up a sibling spat, homework stress or a screaming match like laughter. Take a break! Turn on some music, dance, go outside to play, tell jokes, read a joke book, dress up, make faces, have fun and laugh! Bonus: Your child will think you're the most awesome parent ever!!!!

If you are looking for some more great tips to bring on more patience, download my Patience Playbook, it's free and you can find it at http://bit.ly/patienceplaybook.

SECTION 2
COMMUNICATION & ATTITUDE

Ten

COMMUNICATION: WHERE IT ALL BEGINS

Communication is a vital part of every family and it starts when your child is born. Without communication, the family unit falls apart. Instead of being a family, you become a group of individuals living together, basically roommates. That is, roommates who don't talk to each other. So, let's get started creating a family for you that talks together, listens to each other, laughs together and enjoys each other's company whenever and wherever.

First, we will address where to communicate and then we will move on to how to communicate.

THE WHERE

Communication can, and should, happen whenever you are all together and around each other. That's not to say there isn't time to ponder without feeling like you have to talk to each other. When there is something to be said, we want everyone feeling comfortable and secure enough to speak.

FAMILY MEETINGS

The Family Meeting, discussed in more detail in Chapter 4, is key to creating an atmosphere of respect and calm communication in your family. Weekly Family Meetings are designed to allow for honest, open discussion about what has been going on over the past week and what we can do to improve, enhance and add to the next week. All discussions take place without criticism or judgement. Family Meetings should also include discussions on the week's schedule ahead as well as compliments of how well your child has been doing. Every Family Meeting should start with a compliment for each of your children, if you have more than one, and you may just be surprised when they share a compliment about you.

FUN

When your family is having fun together, laughing, going on outings and celebrating special occasions; communication comes easily. These moments are the future memories of your child's life. Simply put, do stuff with your child! Enjoy life, run around, read, play tag, go to a park, have a picnic, go to the zoo, go to a playground, have a party! The list is endless for what you and your child can do together. Everything your family does together opens up bridges of communication in a safe, comfortable, relaxed and cooperative environment.

PEACE AND QUIET

Need to have a serious, important discussion about something? Regardless of whether you think it's serious or your child thinks it is, choose a location to talk that is free from interruptions and distractions. Close a door, ask others to leave, whatever you need to do, so that your child feels safe talking to you without the whole world chiming in. Let them speak while you just listen without interruption. This will allow them to open up more and absorb and understand the information you are offering as well.

TURN OFF THE DISTRACTIONS

How do you feel when you are trying to talk to someone and, instead of looking at you, they are busy checking their phone? This sends you the direct message that they think that what you have to say is not important. The same goes for your child. So, turn it all off: the phones, the tablets, the TV, and listen to what your child has to say. Not only will you better understand what they are trying to convey to you, but you are inadvertently teaching them good listening and conversation skills.

LISTEN WITH YOUR EYES

I love this expression because it clearly demonstrates that it does not just take ears to listen, it takes your attention and your ability to sit and look at the person you are conversing with. You should be at your child's level, sitting on chairs or on the floor; or bent down to their height and looking them straight into their eyes. This shows (and teaches) respect for what they have to say and enhances their confidence to talk to you about anything.

TAKE ADVANTAGE OF A CAPTIVE AUDIENCE

There are so many times in a family's life that present us with a captive audience for conversation, so take advantage of it.

The Car Ride

One of the most common times for a captive audience is when you are in the car with your child going somewhere. Avoid turning on the radio and refrain from using your phones and tablets. Start a conversation with your child. Do fun stuff like singing songs together, playing car games like the Alphabet game (where you look outside of the car to find letters A through Z), telling jokes. The goal is to create an atmosphere of speaking to each other when in the car instead of everyone being in their own private world. Car rides are a great way to talk about your day or address any issues that may be on your mind.

Go For a Walk

Going for a walk not only gives everyone a breath of fresh air and much needed Vitamin D from the sun, it also is a great way to exercise and an even better opportunity to talk to each other. So many benefits, so little effort.

Eat Together at the Table

Eat your family meals, especially dinner, together at the table instead of in front of the TV as much as possible. When we eat at a table together, there are so many great benefits. Here are some of them:

1. Eating together elevates happiness and conversation and reduces stress. Eating family meals at a dinner table as often as you can is a great way to talk and laugh more and enjoy each other's company. Studies have proven that children and parents that participate in regular family meals eaten together at a table have less stress and lead a happier life.

2. Control what you eat. Conversation is a natural way to slow the process of eating; the complete opposite of what happens when

you eat in front of the TV. When watching TV, you are focused on a show and not paying attention to what or how much you are eating and you will eat more than you intended to eat, with very little conversation going on.

3. Nutrition is increased. It has been proven that we eat better when we eat together as a family. A 2000 survey found that children who ate dinner with their families tended to eat healthier food options, like fruits and vegetables, and less of the junk that is fried and low in nutrients.

4. Home-cooked dinners save money. When a family dinner is planned, shopped for and prepared, it saves your family money. A family that does not plan home-cooked meals spends more money on carry out meals and delivery.

5. If you're not used to eating together, start with one day at a time and increase as you go to include as many days of the week as possible.

6. If scheduling doesn't allow you to eat together for dinner, choose a meal that works best for your family. Try to avoid scheduling activities that overlap with mealtime.

Eleven

WHO'S IN CHARGE HERE?

YOU ARE!

I'm tempted to end this chapter right here, but I am assuming that the reason you are reading this book is to learn more, so allow me to be clear on this.

I work with so many parents who are torn between wanting their kids to like them all the time and setting up some real boundaries and limits. They will often tell me:

"My child won't like me if I do that. They will cry or throw a fit. They will be mad. Isn't my job to keep them happy?"

Actually, your job is to equip them so that they can grow up to be intelligent, contributing, self-sufficient, thought provoking, fun and happy adults.

Let's take a step back and look at this thing called life. Are you always happy? Do you always get your way? NO! Is there more instant gratification or delayed gratification? Is there disappointment? Are there ups and downs, good days and bad days? YES! YES! And more YES! It's a roller coaster. Welcome to life, where things don't always go your way.

If you continue to parent your child in a manner that will always give them their way, and they never have the opportunity to experience and learn to deal with disappointment, you are doing them a grave injustice. Children need to learn how to deal with life's ups and downs and the little disappointments that will come their way. They need to take a disappointment in stride and move forward from it. They can't be happy 100% of the time; it's impossible. You can be a super happy person like me, but to say I have never had disappointments in my life would be masking the truth. It's impossible for someone to go through life and not know what it's like to not have things go their way.

What happens when your child does not get the opportunity to exercise their disappointment muscle? They continually react by throwing a fit when someone says "no". They scream, they yell, they throw things, they lash out! Why? Because they are used to getting their way whenever they want something. They don't know how to handle the emotion of disappointment when someone tells them "no". They have never learned what to do with that emotion.

This is where you, their parent or caregiver, come into the picture. Your job is to help them understand that sometimes things don't go their way and, when that happens, you can make other choices and decisions. You can come up with new ideas and create a new path. It is an opportunity, not the end of the world.

For toddlers, this means that if someone else is playing with the toy they want, they will need to choose a new toy. As the parent or caregiver, your job is to help them understand that choosing a new toy will give them something to play with while they are waiting for the other child to be finished playing with their first choice. Then when the other child is done, they can use it. Your job is not to talk the other child into giving up the toy they're playing with--that only teaches your child that when they want their way, if they throw a fit, they will get their way. They have now discovered a negative behavior that works to get what they want.

Remember that you are always the one in control of all situations, even though it might not seem like it. Even when you give your child a choice, you are still in charge of the two choices being offered. They are not deciding what or when to choose, you are. Then, you offer them the two choices that you decided on and they get handed back a little control through their ability to make a choice. When you pay attention to what is negotiable in your home and you offer your child two choices to move forward, you give a little control back to them. That control allows your child to understand, listen and cooperate more when they don't have as much control over other situations.

Control is what causes a lot of arguments in childhood--between you and your child, and between multiple children. However, when control is offered to your child through simple decisions that impact their lives, (like giving them two pairs of pants to choose from or choosing whether they want five or seven minutes more to play in the park), then they feel respected. They feel empowered, safe and trusted and they will return the same respect to you when things are non-negotiable.

Twelve

CREATING A KIND, NICE CHILD

Children have a lot of emotions rolling around in their little underdeveloped brains. What they don't have a lot of is compassion, empathy, kindness, self-control, self-regulation, logic; all that stuff that makes us react in different ways to the emotions we are feeling. It's our job as their parents to teach, model and encourage the positive behavior we want to see in our children.

Think of all the people you have encountered in your lifetime. Who are the ones you have gravitated towards? Who are the ones you remember from your childhood? Who are the ones you think about today and wonder where they are, how they are doing? For the most part, other than the ones who stand out in your mind for some grandiose demonstration of aggression, the majority of the ones you remember are the nice ones, the kind ones, the ones who would treat anyone with respect and courtesy. It's no wonder that when I start working with a parent and ask them to name three qualities that they would want for their child as they grow, one choice is almost always to be kind.

In this chapter, we will discuss just that. How, as a parent, you can ensure that your child becomes a kind human. We will talk about various ways that you can encourage them to be kind and compassionate.

First and foremost, in order to raise kind, caring children, you yourself need to be a kind, caring human. If you always have a chip on your shoulder, or you yell easily or you don't share or interact with your child, chances are they will learn to respond to people and situations in the same way. You must be the example of a kind person. You must speak kindly; that means you smile, you use the beautiful words in your language, not the ugly ones. You use your manners and speak age-appropriately and respectfully to your child and to others in your communities and your world. The more that your child witnesses the way you speak to family, friends and perfect strangers, the more they learn what kindness is and how people respond positively to a genuinely pleasant, positive person.

Think of that person, you know, the one that spends their lives trashing other people or always being negative, you want to block them on social media or even block them from your life. When children are surrounded by negative, critical people they wind up blocking themselves and their own emotions. They are unable to block the negative people that surround them, because they're children, and the community they live in is decided upon by their parents. They become a fearful person that feels judged all the time, they feel they are never worthy and that nothing they do is good enough. They learn not to trust themselves or anyone else. The really sad truth is that they grow to hate themselves, not you.

Instead, let's start being pro-active. Let's start creating an environment where kindness is king… where your child can recognize how good it feels to be around a nice person that treats them kindly and respectfully. This allows your child to become the same type of adult that stands before them.

How can you, the parent, make this happen? What can you do to make this a reality?

Watch and observe. When you start to see your child sharing with another child, (for instance, maybe, they bring out two snacks instead of just one, so their friend can also have a snack), take advantage and compliment their behavior. Let them know how considerate that was to think of their friend's needs as well as theirs.

Start sitting down together and talking about different ways that you, as a family, can start implementing random acts of kindness right here in your home. Brainstorm about ways you can show that you love and care about each other. Mention things like volunteering to help with the dishes before you are asked. Picking up your room without a reminder or even making the bed of a sibling just to surprise them. Next, have everyone say something kind about the other family member and mention something nice that someone else did for them. This gets your child in the habit of taking notice of other acts of kindness.

When discussing school, work or daycare, be sure to ask your child daily if someone did something nice for them. Also, ask if they did anything nice for someone else or if something happened to them that made them smile. Introducing a pet into the family is another way to teach your child about compassion, kindness and love for others. A pet not only offers opportunities for increased responsibility, but also allows them to learn to treat another living thing with gentleness and love. It teaches them to recognize the needs that others have and see their world as a bigger picture beyond themselves.

When you and your child practice kindness every day and learn to recognize the kindnesses that others do for you, you create a child who becomes naturally compassionate and has empathy for those around them.

Thirteen

GRATITUDE: CHANGING YOUR 'TUDE

Gratitude...to be grateful, to appreciate, to understand that you are fortunate enough to have things in your life that other people just dream about. Gratitude is the one thing that can change a person's outlook and perspective of the world around them; allowing them to understand that:

"Wow, I AM pretty darn fortunate."

Gratitude is the ability to recognize that there are a lot of people in the world who just dream of having one smidgen of what you have. Maybe it's running water, a roof over your head, a blanket to keep you warm at night or the joy of having your own child; a lot of people only dream of having these things.

When you focus on all the good that you have in your life, you stop focusing on what you don't have. You stop comparing what others have and saying: "I wish I could get the car my neighbor just bought" or "I wish I was able to afford those cool shoes," when there are 30 pairs of shoes, (each of them were pretty cool on the day you bought them), sitting in your closet right now.

This concept of being grateful for what you are fortunate to have will change the way you look at the world. It will change the way your child looks at the world. It will change how all of you feel inside.

CAN A TODDLER BE GRATEFUL?

Absolutely! Toddlers, by nature, believe the world revolves around them, (and a lot of times it does). However, when you start talking about being grateful and using the methods I set forth in this chapter, your toddler will start to learn the importance and benefits of gratitude.

I hear parents always complain about how much laundry they need to do or how the dishes are piled high in the sink; how nobody helps them with getting all of the work done. We address chores and getting them done in Chapter 29. Ok, so there's a lot of stuff piling up in your house, I get it. Now, let's turn it around and look at it from a grateful perspective. You have a lot of laundry because it means you're fortunate enough to have clothes to wear. You have a lot of dishes because it means you're fortunate enough to have food to eat. Are you seeing those piles in a new light? Yes, they're still there. Yes, they still need to be done…but how fortunate you are to have those piles! There are people all over the world who would be thrilled to be in your shoes and have the problem of too many dirty dishes or clothes.

When you begin to see how very fortunate you are and you teach your child to see life from the same perspective, it makes complaining about these obstacles seem a little ridiculous. If you're not happy about all the laundry you have, maybe you can limit the amount of clothes that are worn by giving away some. If there are too many dishes in the sink and your child complains about having to clean them, or help you clean them, then ask them if they would rather give some of that food away to someone who hasn't eaten anything for two days, so there are not so many dishes. Yes, it's an extreme viewpoint, but honestly, it's the truth. It's how you start teaching your child to be grateful for what they have and recognizing how many people in the world do not share their abundance.

Now that you understand how you can hold the viewpoint of seeing the glass half full, recognizing where you are fortunate and not dwelling on what you don't have, you can begin to discuss gratitude and starting every day with a grateful heart and an abundant perspective.

Someone who is grateful cannot act entitled at the same time. These are two ends of the spectrum. Teaching a child to be grateful for what they have in their life will always create a positive outlook and leave the negative behind.

Here are some other fun ways to instill the attitude of gratitude in everyone in your family. Put these tips into practice and watch their view on life change.

1. **Start a family Gratitude Journal.** This is a book that is for the whole family's use, even yours. Every day, have each person write down what they are grateful for. Start with one thing and build to three things per person per day. As they grow to teens, you can have them add 5-10 things each day. If you have a child who doesn't write yet, let them dictate it. At first, they will think of the easy things, like "I am grateful for my mommy and daddy."

"I am grateful for my baby doll." "I am grateful for our dog." However, the more you add your thoughts in, like "I am grateful for the rain, because it makes the world greener and allows the plants to grow", the more your child will learn to look outside of their immediate world and start expanding their thinking. Once this starts happening, you will really begin to see a shift in their mindset and they will learn to appreciate their family, their home, and all of the things they're lucky enough to have and do.

I also recommend that you read over what everyone wrote before they go to bed. You can even have them add one more thought for something they are grateful for that happened to them within the day. This consistency of gratitude allows everyone to go to bed and wake up with a new outlook on life.

2. **Family Meetings (see chapter 4)**. After you have conducted your family meeting and before you are ready to adjourn, go around the table and have each family member say what they are grateful for.

3. **Write Thank-You Notes & help your child explore the joy of giving.** Help your child to show their appreciation for gifts that others have given to them by having them say "Thank You" at the time the gift was given and to follow up with a little note of gratitude. When writing the note, don't let your child stop at, "Thank you for my gift," dive deeper with them. Ask them questions and discuss it. WHY are they grateful for this gift? WHAT do they like about it? Will it help them do something they've always wanted to do? HOW will they use this gift? HOW does the gift make them feel? HOW do they think the person that gave them the gift will feel when they find out how that gift made

them smile? HOW do YOU feel when you give someone a gift? Explore the feelings of giving and even your youngest child will start to understand how important it is to give and make others happy. They will start recognizing how great they feel when they bring another person joy.

4. **Showing your child the reality that other people are dealing with hardship.** As you drive around town, notice if there are homeless people on the street and explain why they live in the park or on a sidewalk. Explain that these people do not have homes and families to go to. They live on the street because they have nowhere else to live.

5. **Volunteer** in soup kitchens, senior facilities, hospitals, homeless shelters and places where your child can interact with and help others in need. Let them feel the warmth that is created by being kind and thoughtful to others.

6. Choose a special **charity** or family to help during holiday time.

7. **Donate!** Go through toys, clothes and clutter and give your excess to those in need. Have your child contribute part of their allowance to a charity fund that the whole family contributes to.

8. **Model Gratitude In All Situations.** Talk to your child about stories of when you, or someone else in the family, recognized how you were able to be grateful in different situations. This is a great time to converse with the elders of your family and to relate to hardships that they had growing up.

I remain passionately grateful for the blessings I have, (and I am not talking about money or materialistic objects).

I am truly grateful to you for reading this book and wanting to make a better life for your child. By doing this, you contribute to my passion of giving every child the opportunity to have a fun childhood, to be their best person and live the life that they want to live. For this I say, "Thank you!"

BONUS

I'd like to add a bonus to this chapter. A few extra things that you can incorporate into your child's life to reinforce the beliefs that your child forms.

In addition to stating what you're grateful for every morning and evening, I would like to add in two more things to include in your morning routine.

1. **Affirmations:**

    Affirmations are statements of what is true for you, not what has been created by the limiting beliefs in your head. Affirmations allow you to start living your purpose and becoming the person you are destined to be. Please be willing to do all of these ideas with your child. The affirmation starts with the two most important words in any language: I AM! I advise you to only follow these two words with positive words, never negative words. Speak life and positive energy into your mind and soul.

Here are examples of positive affirmations:

I AM creative.

I AM beautiful inside and out.

I AM grateful.

I AM wise.

I AM funny.

I AM smart.

I AM helpful.

I AM kind.

I AM worthy.

I AM going to ace my test this afternoon.

I AM going to pass my driver's test.

I AM… you get the idea. Positive, positive, positive… if it doesn't make you smile and puff out your chest after you say it, then it needs an overhaul.

2. **Wouldn't it be AWESOME if…**

We all have dreams and goals, even your child. You want them to dream and believe in themselves. One of the ways they can do that and keep moving forward is to imagine how it feels if what they are dreaming about actually comes true. Maybe you and your husband have been wanting to take a trip together and have been thinking about that for about 5 years…now is the time to speak it into life.

"Wouldn't it be awesome if we went to Hawaii in January!?"

Maybe your child has been practicing for the football team this year. Have them speak that dream into life:

"Wouldn't it be awesome if I was on the football team!?"

Maybe your toddler really wants to learn their colors and has been practicing and practicing. Have them say it!

"Wouldn't it be awesome if I learned my colors!?"

The point is, when you continue to focus on goals and dreams, you become intentional in reaching them because they stay in the forefront of your mind. These "Wouldn't it..." statements create an emotional excitement and commitment to make things come true.

There is an easy way to incorporate all of this into your morning routine every day. I encourage you to make this a three-step empowerment process for everyone in your family. As you continue to do this daily motivation together, you will see the connection between everyone grow stronger and stronger.

Here is a great way to get started:

1. Go to an office supply store or a general store and buy a tri-fold presentation board (it's very handy because it is already set up in three sections).

2. At the top of the left section write I AM in big, bold letters. In the middle section at the top write I AM SO GRATEFUL FOR... and at the top of the right section, write WOULDN'T IT BE AWESOME IF... Or, you can make this board a fun project by using decorative or vinyl letters or print headings off of a computer and have your child help you glue them on. They can also decorate them with stickers and decals.

3. Every morning each member of the family writes one thing under each category. It's great to use different colors for each person so you know who wrote each statement.

4. Put this board somewhere that everyone can see it easily and enjoy reading all of the statements on it. You can even read it together over your family dinner table.

5. Have fun with this. The more fun and laughter you incorporate, the more your child will love doing it. Don't be afraid to add in some really funny goals too.

A grateful heart is a full heart. It becomes a peaceful heart, as well as a heart that appreciates everything that comes its way.

I'll end with a quote from Alyssa Knight (12 years old) that I think sums all of this up rather nicely.

"Count your rainbows, not your thunderstorms."

Fourteen

WHEN YOUR CHILD STOPS LISTENING

"Wow, they used to be so obedient. I would ask them to do something and they would do it. No fights, no yelling, no defiance. What the heck happened?"

Is this what you're thinking? Independence happened, that's what. As your child grows and discovers new abilities every day, one of those skills is their ability to think for themselves and offer or demonstrate their own ideas. Is it frustrating? Sometimes. Is it a good thing? Most of the time. Why?

You have been busy teaching your child new skills and how to be more independent. Well, guess what? It worked!

Your child IS becoming more independent, more reliant on themselves than you. Yes, they're still little. Yes, they still need your guidance, attention, security and love, but now they are discovering that they can do things for themselves. They can start learning to dress themselves, using a fork and spoon on their own, going on the potty and yes, they can start speaking and saying No!

Annoying? Sometimes, (okay, a lot of times). Necessary? Absolutely!

Around the age of two, what many like to call the Terrible Twos, is when toddlers begin to discover their voice, their attitude and their ability to test the boundaries. Simply put, they're growing up. Their little brain is saying to them, "Let's do something different, let's NOT do what Mommy or Daddy says and see what happens." It's actually not terrible; it's life.

What do you do? You bargain, you yell, you ask friends, you ask family, you ask the doctor, you drink, (haha, well, I hope not), and still, nothing works! So, you decide to read this book to help you out. Smart option! Your curiosity is always a good thing. The better you understand, the more cooperation and smiles will take over.

Remember that a toddler is different than a 10-year-old, different than a 15-year-old and most definitely, different than an adult. When talking and reacting to them, this is something you must never forget.

Simply put, they're testing their limits and yours. They're seeing just how far you will go until they get their way. This will show up in a variety of ways: yelling, ignoring you, doing the opposite of what you ask, throwing things, temper tantrums, crying, whining, fighting with siblings, and running away. They may literally try any method, until one actually works. They get their way and then it becomes the norm.

How do they figure out what works, you ask? When you give into their demands, you confirm for them that the specific method they just used worked. They will continue to use that as long as it is successful. So yes, it's all dependent on you and your reaction. If your child is whining and you acknowledge it by giving into their request, they will continue to whine. If every time they throw a temper tantrum, they get their way, they will continue to throw temper tantrums. It is really quite simple; however, it is never easy.

WHAT CAN YOU DO?

First of all, if they are testing a boundary that you have set up for them, stick to your guns and don't give in. Regardless of how they react, you stay firm.

For example: You tell your child that after this book it is time to go to sleep and you will turn the lights out. At the end of the story, they ask for one more book. If you reply with "OK, just one more and then lights out", you have just confirmed a "testing the limits" method that works. The result of you saying ok to this request, is that they will now feel comfortable asking for just one more and will "ONE MORE…" you to death. One more book, one more drink of water, one more kiss, one more hug, one more song, one more…, one more…, one more.

STOP THE NONSENSE NOW!

When they say, "one more…" you say:

> "I'm sorry, honey, we will read more books tomorrow. It is time to go to sleep. I'll see you in the morning."

Then, leave. Walk out the door, turn out the lights, let them go to bed, even if they're screaming.

> "Mommy, just one more book, pleeeeeeeze."

Don't give in, keep walking; it will all stop when they realize it didn't work. When you stay consistent with your boundaries and don't give in, they will understand the boundaries are firm and follow them as well.

Hey, there's no harm in trying, and this is not to say that they won't try it a few more times, but your job is to stay consistent with your response every time. Once you give in, you give them permission to keep acting that way. They will do it again and again, and you will need to start all over with being consistent with your boundaries to get the behavior to stop.

THEIR RESPONSES AND WHAT YOU SHOULD DO
So, let's review what to do when they react in different ways to a request; when they are told "no" or when they are not given something they want.

THEY CRY or THROW A TEMPER TANTRUM*... Let them cry! Crying never hurt anyone. After they calm down (and they will fairly quickly once they see that you are not reacting to their tears) you can sit down with them and explain why they didn't get their way.
*See Chapter 35 on Temper Tantrums.

THEY WHINE
Don't give in if they are speaking to you in a whiny voice. Tell them any one of these things: "If you want to tell me something, you need to smile when you're talking," or "Please speak nicely and I will be happy to help you," or simply, "Let's try that again." Any of these will work as a response, but afterwards, go back to what you were doing and/or walk away until they speak to you nicely. Don't keep repeating the same response. Stay consistent with this and eventually, the times they whine to you will be fewer (HINT: you need to model kind speech

as well. Be calm and smile when YOU talk and they will react in the same way).

NON-NEGOTIABLES (see Empowerment Chapter 24): When something is a non negotiable, like bedtime or the time you need to leave in the morning or when they need to take a bath, stop asking them and just do it. Never ask your child a question that can be answered with a NO if 'no' is not an option.

Example: "Logan, in five minutes it's time to get in your bath."

Assuming you have a bedtime routine in place, bath time is not going to be a surprise for Logan. He should understand and cooperate. If he decides to fight you on stopping his playing, try this:

"Logan, it's time for your bath, you can play for four or seven more minutes. How much longer would you like to play?"

Now many toddlers, who don't really understand time, may ask you back:

"Which is longer?"

You tell them seven minutes and that will usually be the answer they choose. Then tell them:

"I'll set a timer and when it goes off, it's time to get into the tub."

When you give your child power over what is negotiable, they become more cooperative when things are non-negotiable.

Important reminder: Never ask your child a question that can be answered with a response of no, if no is not an option. If you are asking a Yes or No question to something that is not negotiable, (like a time you have to leave or something that they must do), you actually do more harm than good. This is because you are offering a choice, which is a way to empower them, but then you are disregarding their answer, which is how you get your child to start believing that you don't care about what they have to say. However, if no is a valid option for them, then ask and if they say no, let that be ok. Don't be afraid of your child's assertiveness; it is a good thing and will serve them well as they grow into adulthood. Remember, through all of this, your goal is to raise a well-rounded, thoughtful, strong, empowered, happy adult. However, boundaries need to be set to achieve this. Children who always get their way, regardless of the situation, will become entitled, whiney, screaming children and this behavior will continue into their adulthood. Your child needs to learn how to deal with disappointment. Basically, you're not doing your child any favors by giving into their every demand.

You're still the boss; you're still in charge. Allow them to test the limits, grow and be more independent. Offer them control over negotiations and they will be willing to cooperate when they need to. After all, your child really wants to please you, even though it doesn't always seem that way. Their growing independence and their knowledge of their boundaries and limits are good things and will help them see what life has to offer. They will begin to understand that sometimes things don't go their way and that's okay.

Fifteen

ONE & DONE! OR "IF I DON'T YELL, THEY DON'T LISTEN!

No one feels good about yelling, especially when we are yelling at our child. When we lose our temper, we lose control. So how does it happen when we try our best to stay calm? Triggers, plain and simple. Those triggers may be contributing to the way you are feeling or the way your child is feeling. Did we have a really bad day, are we tired, hungry, thirsty, frustrated, overwhelmed? Triggers send us into behaviors that are emotionally driven and not thought based. Sometimes, there are things that your child may do that will simply set you off.

For example, I consider myself a pretty calm, level-headed person; however, if someone calls me a liar or accuses me of lying, I explode; I literally shake, and my heart rate absolutely increases. I pride myself on being a person of integrity and do my best to tell the truth wherever and whenever I do anything. So, when someone accuses me of not telling the truth, I simply lose it and I go off defending my truth.

When parenting, there is a common event that causes most parents to lose their cool and yell. By far, the reason most parents go from calm to screaming is having to repeat the same request multiple times and ultimately finding the need to yell to get the job done.

You're going about your regular day and you ask your child to stop playing and come eat dinner, and the next thing you know everyone is yelling, aggravated and you can't even sit down to a relaxing meal. You think, "How did this happen, I always have to yell to get this child to do anything? Why doesn't he just listen the first time I ask?"

Well, as you may or may not have assumed, this issue is very common to almost everybody that I ask.

"Why do you yell?"

All parents say, "I yell because I ask my child over and over to do something and only after I start yelling does it finally get done. If I don't yell, they don't listen!"

So, let's address this right now, because this will be one of the biggest changes you make in your own parenting and an essential strategy to increase calm and cooperation.

I guarantee that all of you have experienced this problem at one time or another. I used to do the same thing when my children were young and then I realized the problem was not them, it was me. I needed to change my ways and make the decision to stop asking over and over again. This is how I did it.

But first, let's examine this problem deeper and really analyze it. Every time you ask something of your child, you need to ask them over and over and over, until you get so aggravated and frustrated that you explode, and then they finally do what they're told. Does that sound about right?

Is the problem that you are exploding, or is the problem that you're asking your child over and over again? We're going to stop that habit and then we can stop yelling, okay? I'm going to help you stop it.

What if you could ask your child once or twice and then they did what you asked? What if you would never get to the point of yelling? How would that feel? How would the atmosphere be in your home, calmer, more relaxed? Take a minute and think how great it really would be.

So, how about we make that happen by changing this behavior? The good news is, by changing your behavior you will change your child's.

Now, let's talk a little bit about how you actually accomplish this. I hate to tell you, but you have trained your child to wait for the third or fourth time…to actually wait for you to yell before they respond. You have actually trained them to do this. What??? I know; it sounds crazy. Can you imagine? If you were able to just ask them one time and they would actually follow through? You're thinking, "Well, maybe in someone else's house." I'm talking about your house and YES it can happen for you.

Ready to learn how? Okay! I like to call it one and done. Could be two and done, but that's the most I'm giving you. One and done or two and done. Let me offer this scenario. I always like to use a tablet or video games as my example because these are very common struggles. For this example, we will talk about their tablet. Your child is playing on their tablet and you are fixing dinner. You walk in to where they're playing and say very calmly and politely:

"Please turn off your tablet and come eat dinner."

Then you walk away to continue working on dinner. Your child, however, does not turn off the tablet and continues to play. You're gone, so they're playing. You come back five minutes later.

"I asked you to please stop playing on your tablet so we can eat dinner. Now, turn it off."

Then you walk away. They continue playing on the tablet…playing, playing, playing. You come back five minutes later and declare:

"I'm really getting irritated, please stop playing on your tablet and come in to eat."

You walk away, they continue to play. Now you walk in for the final time, you've lost it and you start screaming.

"I'm sick of telling you to get off this tablet; I'm ready to throw it in the garbage. It is time to eat!"

You grab the tablet and maybe their arm and escort them to dinner, once again confirming your belief that if you don't yell, they don't listen.

Now let's examine what happened. You came in the first time and you said, "Please stop playing on the tablet and come eat dinner." You reflect: I'm being a wonderful parent, I'm using my manners and staying calm.

Then you walk away. Here's the first problem: when giving instruction to a toddler, stay within their sightline to assure the job is done. For toddlers out of sight, out of mind is 100% true. When you walk away, they get easily distracted and continue doing what they were doing before you came in.

In this scenario, you walked away and expected your child to do what you asked. That's not what happened and instead they kept playing. Five minutes later, you came back. Then repeated it three more times. Well, your child has now had 5, 10, 15 additional minutes to play on their tablet before you came in and yelled. Why? Because they are learning, (or you can say being trained), to wait until you come in and scream before reacting. They have learned that nothing really happens until you yell and, in reality, they are rewarded with additional playtime while they wait for you to scream. You kept walking away, no one was watching, so they kept playing. Here is where you are training them to behave this way now and for the rest of their years of childhood. They are being trained every time this happens. That's why they don't listen, because you have trained them not to.

Now let's create a new scenario, and we'll look at three different ways to react.

First scenario, you come in to talk to your child calmly and ask:

"Would you please stop playing on your tablet, and come eat dinner?"

Now, suppose you walk away and go back into the kitchen. Your child still continues to play on their tablet, (which they will because this is how it's always been done). They're about to find out that today will be different. After all, you have to start doing things differently, (that's why you're reading this book), and today is a great day to start. So, here it is: your first day of doing something different. This time, you enter the room where your child is playing on their tablet and, instead of yelling, you calmly say:

"I asked you to stop playing. It's dinner time, we need to go eat."

Tablets are extremely portable which makes this scenario a whole lot easier. You add in your nice, calm voice, "I will be taking the tablet from you for the rest of the evening and you can have it back tomorrow. However, if you continue to not listen when I ask you to turn off your tablet, I will continue to take it away. I will do this until you decide to turn it off when I ask you to."

You take the tablet away and go eat dinner. One and done! I know what you're thinking, if I take away their tablet, my child will start screaming like the world has ended. To this I say: let them. Ignore the tantrum and walk away to eat dinner. Do not give in! Do not give the tablet back! Do not, do not, do not!! Habits are not easy to break, and this is basically a habit. Walk away and eat your dinner. The tantrum will only last forever if you react to it, so don't, (see Chapter 35 on tantrums).

In the second scenario, you negotiate. End times of play can become one of the negotiations you offer your child to give them back a little control over their life. Here's how it goes. It's about 15 minutes before you are ready to sit down and eat. This time you come in and say to your child:

"It's almost dinner time, would you like three or five more minutes to play on your tablet?"

Allow your child to choose their end time and tell them you will set the alarm. When the alarm rings, remind your child that time is up and to come in for dinner. Quite often, that's all they need; since they set the time limit, they will take responsibility for their actions. If they don't stop, however, go back to the last paragraph, where you then take the tablet away.

For example, my three year old grandson is so used to me asking him time options and setting alarms for end times, he now asks for the alarm to be set for a lot of things. He even asks his mom to set her alarm at work, so she comes home on time.

In the third scenario, you come into where your child is playing, and you ask them to stop playing and come eat. This time you stay within their eyesight, watching them until they put the tablet down and come in. Kids want to ultimately please their parents and if you're standing there, they will usually do as you ask, sometimes with the help of your coaching. They will stop without you having to yell and move on to the next request.

Just remember, even if it doesn't work the first time, that doesn't mean it will not work. Do not give up, stay consistent and you will find success.

For all these scenarios, don't forget to acknowledge the good behavior they have exhibited so that they know you have noticed, and they have done something you're proud of.

Sixteen

WHEN CHILDREN BEND THE TRUTH & LIE

First of all, let me start out with how much I don't like the word 'lie'. Part of it is, I get hugely defensive when someone calls me a liar, as I consider myself to be a person of integrity and truth. The other part is that I feel like it is very aggressive, accusatory and often without merit. While many will read this chapter and think, oh this chapter is about lying; it is, but the language I use will be the reverse. That language will be when your child is 'not telling the truth.'

Let's talk about verbiage for a moment. The way you speak to your child can be either encouraging and helpful in engaging them in conversation, or it can be accusatory and result in them being defensive and defiant. Here are a few examples of how you can state that you think your child might be lying without actually saying it or shoving it in their face. Questions like:

"Are you telling the truth?" or "Are you sure that this is how it happened?" or "Thanks for telling me what happened, is there anything you forgot to tell me?" all sound much less threatening. Once you have gotten to the core of the issue, you can then thank your child for telling the truth. Positive, calm and encouraging language will ALWAYS get you farther than negative accusations.

THE WHY

Let's get into why children turn to fabricating the truth. First off, due to their active imaginations and the fact that they are children, (and learning and growing daily), fabricating stories and engaging in creative, imaginative play with dolls, stuffed animals and other play toys not only comes naturally, it is encouraged by their parents and other caregivers. A fabricated story, whether it is about a doll or during a situation when the child might think they are going to get in trouble, it is still a fabricated story. Your child doesn't know the difference at this point, or when one is permitted and one is not. They learn this distinction from you.

As toddlers get a bit older, around two to four years, they realize that if they fabricate a story about something they are being accused of, this story may save them from being punished. This is when they start to bend the truth to their advantage.

Another reason that children decide to not tell the truth is because their answer to a question may be I don't know. Since they are unsure if that is an acceptable answer, they fabricate an answer that they think may work better. In addition, your child may lie if they don't know the answer, because they might be embarrassed or uncomfortable that they don't know, so they make something up.

Your child may start to move away from stating the truth because they see role models, (their parents or their siblings), doing it and they think they can do it too.

Lastly, they stretch the truth because they have been given permission to lie. When an adult asks a child to keep a secret, or asks them not to tell Dad or Mom, they are indirectly giving that child permission to lie. When someone calls or comes to the door and the child hears their parent say, tell them I'm not here, they just gave that child permission to lie.

Hopefully, this now gives you a little insight into why children learn to alter the truth and why they don't start doing it to be irritating or mean to you. They do it because they are getting more creative mentally, they are understanding concepts more, and, very often, they may be just modeling someone else's behavior.

What do you do now? Your child has begun to tell you stories instead of the truth. How do you turn it around, so it doesn't become a habit or an even greater issue?

THE SAFE HOUSE

First, I want you to talk to your child about the fact that your house is a safe house. Allow them to feel confident, that they can say and talk to you about anything. However, in order for you to give them that confidence, you need to be a good listener, (refer to Chapter 10 on Communication). In order to be a good listener, you need to listen completely; you don't judge, you don't criticize, you just advise. You create an all-in attitude for everyone in your family concerning telling the truth. It becomes your culture, your behavior and the way you live as a role model for your child. If you can't do this, they will not feel comfortable talking to you and the fabrication and lies will continue.

CONSEQUENCES

Consequences are a part of life and are the results of the choices we make. This is an important lesson to teach your child. Consequences need to be decided before the incident presents itself, if at all possible, or very soon after the first time the problem occurs.

In this case, what will happen if the lies continue? Will you offer them some time to sit and think about what they are saying? Will you discuss what they are saying versus what you know is the truth? Will you both do some research on the subject?

Harsh discipline is not suggested as it has been proven that children who are harshly disciplined for stretching the truth tend to lie more to avoid punishment. In addition, with toddlers, they are just crafting stories that they have been encouraged to do through play and using their imagination. Your child is in need of guidance to learn the difference between fantasy and reality. This difference is not something that is planted in their brain from birth.

WE ALL MAKE MISTAKES

It is important to help your child understand that making mistakes is not a bad thing. Mistakes are bumps in the road that teach us to be more flexible, encourage problem solving and conflict resolution. All successful humans have made many mistakes to get to where they are in life. In fact, every human makes mistakes and, since we are all human, we all make mistakes.

This may be a great time to share with your child some of the mistakes you have made and how you have dealt with them. When they tell a fib as a toddler, because they have learned to fabricate stories through play, they are essentially making a mistake. It is your job as their parent to start teaching them what is reality and what is fantasy. To help them understand that, when you make a mistake, it is not the end of the world. In fact, mistakes are great teaching moments and should be welcomed.

You can also talk about all the great products we enjoy that were generated by a mistake. Some of these mistakes resulted in items that we would find it hard to live without. Play- Doh®, Post-It® Notes and the light bulb were all technically created through errors. Along with your child, look up the history of products like these and talk about how they were created. The more you talk about how mistakes can positively affect your life, and the more your reaction to their mistakes is calm and accepting, the less emotional your toddler will get when they make one.

NEGOTIABLES & NON-NEGOTIABLES

There are things in our lives, our household, our schedules and our routines that are negotiable and non-negotiable. For example, the time you must be in the car to get to school on time is a non-negotiable. Whether your child wears the red pants or the blue pants is negotiable. Why is this important? Because the more opportunity that you give your child to make their own choices, the more you will empower them and build their trust and confidence. This will create more cooperation when something is not negotiable. The more cooperation, the more gets done and the need for fabricating stories is lessened.

UNDERSTANDING THE LIE

As you try to get to the bottom of their story, it is helpful for you to really understand why they felt the need to lie.

First, what was the lie about? Did they say they did something, when clearly they did not? For example, did they say they brushed their teeth when you know they didn't because their toothbrush is dry? Did they take something and claim they didn't?

It is important to understand the WHAT and the WHY. Clearly, if they did do something that could be dangerous, like plugging a cord into the wall, the danger of this is evident and must be addressed immediately. However, if the child denied brushing their teeth, that can be easily discussed due to the fact that their toothbrush is dry. You can talk to your child calmly about the importance of brushing and ways that they can ensure they brush every day. Really understand what they did, why they did it and how you can address the issue in as calm a response as possible.

Your child's understanding of fabricating stories to avoid getting in trouble can start as early as two and as old as four. In order to tell an outright lie, a child needs to know the difference between truth and not telling the truth. They need to know the difference between fantasy and reality. All of these are learned behaviors, not behaviors that they are born with. What should you do when your child begins to alter the truth?

Stay calm and speak calmly to them about what the reality of the situation is. Show them the proof if you are able to. If you are not sure your child is lying, don't assume. Always give your child the benefit of the doubt until you learn more about the situation. They might just be telling the truth after all.

Use storytelling as a tool to help them explain what happened. Offer to draw pictures about it with their help.

Help them to understand the difference between fantasy and reality by reading stories and sharing stories that demonstrate the difference. Talk about shows like cartoons and explain that a cartoon character is merely a drawing and not a real being.

A good example of a child's understanding of fantasy and reality just happened the other day. My three year old grandson was watching Sesame Street® and he noticed that Elmo's eyes were not moving. He asked me why and I told him because Elmo was a puppet and was not real. He then said,

"Well, his mouth is moving and he is talking, so he must be real."

Here, you can see his confusion and his inability to differentiate between reality and fantasy. I picked up one of his puppets to demonstrate how puppets work. However, even with this demonstration, it may take him a while to recognize the difference when he sees something like Elmo on TV that just looks so realistic.

Continue to explain to your child about why it is important to tell the truth and be a role model for honesty and integrity. Ultimately, children want to please their parents. When you take notice and compliment them for behaviors that you want them to adhere to, those are the behaviors that they will continue to do in order to make you happy and proud of them.

Remember, when your child pretends, they are essentially not telling the truth. They are learning through playing with dolls and toys to use their imagination to create their own stories and scenarios. In a child's mind, this is a perfectly acceptable and encouraged tool to use in play. The problem is, there are times in life when it is acceptable and when it is not. It is your job as their parent to help them understand and recognize the difference.

Seventeen

TALKING BACK: THE SYMPTOM OF GROWING INDEPENDENCE

Your toddler has learned to speak, they are forming sentences, they understand more, they say more, and they are now testing the waters and speaking up for themselves. Good or bad, most of the time, parents don't like it.

Let's start with why it's good and then we will discuss how you can limit your child's backtalk.

Talking back is a sign of growth and testing limits. It is also a sign of an increased sense of confidence and independence. Your child has figured out how to speak their mind and as far as becoming a secure, confident adult, this is a good thing. You want your child to stand up for themselves in this big, crazy world they are entering. What you don't want is your child standing up for themselves in a disrespectful manner. In my eyes, respect is earned and should always be displayed when speaking to another human being. This includes the way you model respect by the way that you speak to your child and others.

What can you do to ensure your child's confidence and understanding that they do have a say in things? How do you teach them that there is a time and a place for everything, and all things should be done respectfully?

1. Remain calm when your child talks back. Remember that they are responding a lot from emotion and less from understanding the proper way to communicate their feelings. Your ability to stay calm indirectly teaches them to do the same.

2. Reiterate the way you speak to each other in your home, using kindness and manners and showing respect for the other person. Remind them to smile when they speak and use their manners.

3. Continue to hold Family Meetings (Chapter 4) and address the issue of talking back at your next meeting.

4. Be pro-active and establish consequences for talking back prior to the incident happening.

Here' an example of technique 3 and 4 above. One of my clients had a problem with their 5-year-old talking back. Under my advisement, she held her family meeting, discussed the issue and her son decided that if he talked back to his parents, they should put him into a 15-minute time out. Now, although this was a harsher consequence than his parents would have put into place, she took my advice of letting her son decide the consequence and they agreed that this is what would happen. The next time, he started to talk back, he stopped himself, and spoke in a much more respectful way to his mom. Problem solved and with consistency, has not been a major issue since. You see, when children decide their own consequences for choices, and those consequences are implemented, it encourages them to start thinking before they act. This is the beauty of all of this work, to get all of you to think before you react.

You only need to remind your child one time of how we speak in this family, and that they should try it again and use kind words instead. If they repeat the same statement again disrespectfully, then the consequence you decided on is put into action.

5. Recognize and compliment your child whenever they do speak kindly and politely so that they understand that this is an acceptable way to communicate, while the harsh speech is not. Although, I don't expect you to do this everytime they talk, but when it really stands out, make sure you say something like, "Thank you for asking so nicely." This is super important!!

6. If the aggressive statements continue and they are not willing to speak to you kindly, then let them know that you will not respond. Do not give them attention until they speak to you kindly.

7. If they get angry through all of this, then let them calm down before you explain why you were not responding. Do not escalate their behavior by yelling back. If you stay calm, eventually they will calm down too.

It is always important to remember that you are their role model. You are the one setting the boundaries and limits. In addition, you are their coach and the one that is there to teach them how to regulate their emotions and help them reach for calmer, more polite ways to offer up their opinions and feelings. Recognize their feelings, but do not allow your child to be disrespectful. A child that is allowed to disrespect their parents will feel justified in disrespecting anyone.

SECTION 3

FUN
&
LEARNING

Eighteen

PLAYTIME: IT'S NOT JUST A GAME, IT'S AN EDUCATION

"Play is the highest form of research."

~ Albert Einstein

If you ask a parent what are the top three most important jobs you have as a parent other than feeding your child, the majority will tell you to LOVE my child, to TEACH my child and to keep my child SAFE. All true. However, the ways that parents go about doing these are all different, especially teaching.

In this day and age, teaching a child might come from the Internet, videos, video games and other electronic caretakers. To help all of you out, I wanted to write a chapter on the single most important way that your toddler learns, and that is through hands-on PLAY. Whether they are playing with you, someone else or enjoying their own company, your child will not just be having fun, but will be taking in every skill they need to grow, learn and develop.

WHY PLAY

The following is a list of benefits of hands-on and active play. The value is endless; the bond you will form with each other is real, and the fun is never-ending.

Here is the very long list of VALUABLE BENEFITS a child gains from hands-on and active play.

1. Fun and Laughter
2. Fitness
3. Heart health
4. A variety of physical skills like balance & coordination
5. Social skills
6. Cognitive skills
7. Emotional development
8. Language development
9. Fine motor skills
10. Gross motor skills
11. Cooperation skills
12. Creativity
13. Imagination enhancement
14. Understanding and following instructions
15. Taking turns
16. Conflict resolution
17. Problem solving
18. Strategizing
19. Role play
20. Storytelling
21. Self-regulation
22. Spacial awareness

23. Empathy and Compassion

24. Learning a variety of concepts like colors, shapes, letters & numbers

25. Leadership

26. Independence

27. Memory Enhancement

28. Sequencing (the beginnings of Mathematics)

29. Body awareness

30. Mindfulness

31. Confidence

32. Self-worth

33. Self-esteem

34. Self-image

They learn all of these things and there are probably ones I've missed. All of these benefits of active and hands-on play help develop, educate and boost your child's skills more completely and age-appropriately than any activity. It's all accomplished through having fun!

WHAT TO DO WITH YOUR CHILD

There are so many ways to play with your child that I can't possibly list them all. Here are some ideas to get you started. The more creative you are, the more you allow your own inner child to shine, the more fun everyone will have playing together. Here are some ideas to get you started.

1. MUSIC and DANCING are fun activities for everyone and a great way to break up a sibling argument or a tantrum. Ignore what the child is doing, turn on some loud music and start dancing. I guarantee your child will be joining within minutes and the chaotic situation will turn into fun!

2. Pull out some great BOARD GAMES and play together as a family. Have a game night each week and turn those electronics off. All board games have age ratings on them for maximum understanding and enjoyment.

3. BUILDING TOYS and BLOCKS stimulate thought, creativity, abstract thinking and bring on the fun.

4. PUZZLES are a perfect way to teach delayed gratification, as well as strategic planning and abstract thinking.

5. CARD GAMES stimulate the mind, strategic thinking, conflict resolution, develop math skills, are portable and fun!

6. Play DRESS UP and put on a show for the rest of the family. Video the show for everyone to watch later.

7. Have a PICNIC in the park or the backyard, no electronics allowed.

8. PLAY OUTSIDE and enjoy fun, active games in the backyard or park. Tag, catch, dodgeball, red light/green light, freeze and move games, hockey, baseball, basketball (you can use a bucket if you don't have a net), etc. Or make up your own game! Kids are great at it. Exercising in the fresh air and sunshine (Vitamin D) is a health benefit for all and a great stress reducer.

9. Schedule a GIRLS OR BOYS DAY OUT for just you and your child and plan some fun one-on-one activities.

10. Go to THE ZOO or YOUR LOCAL PET STORE. Lots of walking, lots of looking, lots of learning and lots of fun. Kids love animals.

11. Live near an AIRPORT? Most International Airports have viewing areas with parks and playgrounds too. Plan a trip to play while watching the airplanes come in.

12. Go to a SCHOOL PLAYGROUND and spend some time climbing, sliding and swinging.

13. Need stuff? Head to THE MALL, most have indoor play areas for kids, too. This also makes a great outing for a rainy day.

14. Keep this FUN STUFF AT HOME for rainy days or indoor play:
    a. Balloons (under-inflated to avoid popping)
    b. Swimming noodles (cut them in half to 3' for easy and fun toddler play where they can bop around balloons or beach balls)
    c. Foam balls
    d. Small hula-hoops
    e. Tunnels
    f. Mats
    g. Soft balance beams
    h. Cones
    i. Scarves or ribbons for dancing and catching

15. CRAFTS: clay, Play-Doh®, paint, crayons, tape, safety scissors, glue sticks, magazines for collages, toilet paper roll inserts, sidewalk chalk and more. The more you have, the more fun stuff you can create.

16. Have theme days - Pirate day, Superhero day, Earth Day, Dinosaur Day, etc.

17. Bring on the LAUGHTER, it really is the best medicine.

Important note: Just 10-15 minutes of one-on-one playtime with your child (done sporadically throughout the day), is all they need to feel confident to play on their own when you have things to do.

When you make active and hands-on play a part of your everyday life with your toddler, you are giving your child a complete education, an appreciation for each other, an engaging day full of activity and a lifetime love for physical fitness, learning and fun.

Nineteen

READING: THE GATEWAY TO LANGUAGE

Did you know that ReadAloud.org did a National Survey of 1,000 parents to learn how often they read to their children each day? They found that only 30% had daily reading time. That 30% who do read to their children spent, on average, 15 minutes reading. Wow! I don't know about you, but that blows me away. Reading is such a special, intimate time with your child, that I don't know why all parents don't spend some part of their day with a book in their hand and a child on their lap.

Which brings me to a question that I am often asked by parents who have children who are not talking too much by age 2.5.

"What can I do to get my child to talk more? Is there a physical or mental problem that my child has that needs to be addressed? Should I have my child tested?"

The first question I ask those parents is: "Do you read to your child?" The answer is most always, "not really."

I have to say; I know that answer before they even tell me. Reading to your child is one of the most important factors in language development. If you want your child to start talking, you need to start reading to them every day, multiple times a day if at all possible.

Teaching your child the language they need to know will, of course, happen through conversation. It will greatly accelerate and expand their vocabulary when they are consistently read to, and again as they start reading on their own.

Aside from language development, there are many benefits to reading with your child. First off, there is a close bond that happens when a parent and child share a story. It's intimate, peaceful and a time that your child recognizes as solely theirs. Stories take your child on an adventure right in their own home. It expands their imagination, curiosity and excitement for learning new things.

There is considerable cognitive development that comes from reading books, as well as enhancing memory function, compassion, empathy and learning about how feelings are handled in a variety of situations. Reading has also been proven to enhance a child's concentration and focus. So, if you're thinking that your child can't sit still long enough to read, try doing it anyway with them more often. They will learn to focus for longer periods of time. Start with picture books or short books and then increase the size of the stories as they grow. Another wonderful benefit of books is that they help your child reduce stress, allowing them to be calmer and more relaxed.

Reading targeted books can help your child learn new habits like potty-training and break old habits like thumb sucking. There is literally a book for almost anything you want your child to learn or understand. After you have read to your child, you can talk about what was discussed in the book.

One word of advice though; if your child interrupts the story to point out a picture that they like or they have a question, please use that as a teaching moment to discuss what caught their attention. Refrain from telling them that you need to finish the book first and then you can discuss it after. Talk about it right then and there and help them understand what they are curious about. This will also develop their comprehension, which will come in handy as they grow, continue through school and start reading more complex books.

HOW YOU CAN FIT IN AN EXTRA BOOK EACH DAY

Choose and create quiet times throughout your day to add in a book. You can read at bedtime or when they wake up in the morning. You can read books during meals or simply when you need them to settle down for some reason. Need to take a break from your work? Spend 5-10 minutes and read a book with your child. It will refresh you and mean the world to them.

Books make great travel companions. They are small, lightweight and easily portable. Instead of bringing along a tablet in the car, bring some books. Schedule in library time every week. Your child will love reading a book at the library, as well as being able to choose new books to take home. Party tip: Need a present for a child? Every parent welcomes a new book. Need a party favor? Go to the Dollar Store and buy each child a book, wrap them up or put them in a basket and let each child choose one. No one throws away a book like they do the random little toys that come in goody bags.

YOUR HOME

Set up your home as an environment for learning and reading. Have books, comic books and magazines easily accessible on tables, shelves and play areas, so that your child can pick up something to read at any time. Be a reader yourself and share stories with your child.
Here are some great books to read to your child, (that also offer wonderful life lessons):

Toddlers:
- The Itsy Bitsy Spider - a tale of empowerment with a "not giving up" attitude
- Ferdinand - a story about a bull that wants to do his own thing and not follow the others. He has a supportive Mom who is willing to allow him that freedom
- The Little Engine that Could - also a story of not giving up
- The Madeline Series - All about a little girl that likes to stand up and show the world what she has to offer

Other great books as kids grow...
- Superhero stories
- Biographies on people that went above and beyond
- Matilda by Roald Dahl (for that matter, all Roald Dahl books)
- Keys 4 Success for Kids by Caleb Maddix

Take note of your child's interests and find books that relate. What were your favorite books when you were growing up? Start there and share them with your child. As they grow, you can also create a family book club or a neighborhood book club to read and discuss the books together. Lastly, I want to remind you that no one is ever too old to read along with or to read aloud. The bonding is real, the education is enhanced, the memories and love will last a lifetime. Enjoy this time with your child and get started on a new adventure, brought to you by your favorite book!

Twenty

SOCIAL LIFE: DISCOVERING A WORLD OUTSIDE OF THEIR OWN

Very often, parents think the worst of things. If someone comes near my child, they may be sick, they could spread germs; how can I keep them safe? The answer in their mind is to have limited contact with the public. Is that good for your child? Is that really what's best for them?

Providing a healthy social life for your child gives them a myriad of benefits. First and foremost, they begin to make friends. They discover there are other small humans in the world--who are not only their size, but think, smell, sound, act and look like them! They discover that they like the same things and have similar toys that your child wants to play with too. It's a whole new exciting world for them. Yes, there are germs. Yes, both grown-ups and children can spread germs, but how will your child build their immunities without a good dose of some slimy germs?

"A baby's brain needs stimulation, input and interaction to evolve normally, the young immune system is strengthened by exposure to everyday germs so that it can learn to adapt and regulate itself," notes Thom McDade PhD, associate professor and Director of the Laboratory for Human Biology Research at Northwestern University. What they have found, further in their studies, is that when we overly sanitize our child's environment to protect them from illness, we may be depriving them the chance to build a strong immune system and they may actually have increased illnesses now and throughout their lives.

With that said, you should still be careful not to expose them to major illnesses like the flu or other highly contagious diseases. Just remember, don't go overboard with constantly cleansing their hands with hand sanitizer at every corner. They need to be exposed to everyday germs that cause them no danger, but can, in fact, offer them a lifetime of benefits.

Here's an example of going overboard on the exposure and who did it? Me! When my two kids were very little, their best friend had chicken pox. So, I thought it would be a great idea if my kids got it at the same time; assuming they would be getting chicken pox at some point anyway. Here was my plan. All three of them, (Lauren, Kyle and BFF), would bathe together. What better way to expose them than in a bathtub? Well, this was not a really great idea after all. Lauren did get chicken pox and poor Kyle, who was only about two or three, was covered in them from head to toe. Turns out pouring chicken pox infected water all over this poor child, and having him soak in it, was not my best parenting idea. When I took them to the doctor, although I had accomplished my mission of giving them the highly contagious disease, the doctor said he would not have recommended that exorbitant amount of exposure. Well, like I said, we all make mistakes as parents, even me. Now, there is a vaccine for CP, so get it and be done.

Creating a healthy social life for your child will contribute to their exposure to everyday germs, as well as offer them many other healthy physical, cognitive and emotional benefits.

Toddlers learn best through play, (see Chapter 18). They gain a variety of skills from social play as well as individual play. Toddlers gain a multitude of benefits from associating with other children. Humans are naturally social creatures. We find comfort and excitement when we are interacting with others; this is true for toddlers as well.

When toddlers start interacting with other children their same age, they develop speech and learn how to share their space. If your child is under two and playing with other children, their play may begin as more individual play than actually interacting with the other child. They may spend more time watching and less time playing together. They may sit side by side, but have no real interaction at all, which at this age is perfectly normal. It even has a name, parallel play, indicating that the kids are parallel to each other, but not interacting.

Around three years of age, they begin to notice their playmate and take interest in what they are doing. You will begin to see how your child starts actually playing with other children. This is how they start to learn how to get along with and make new friends. With interactive or associative play, (as it is called), they learn that the world doesn't solely revolve around them and they start to recognize emotions and feelings like compassion, kindness, empathy, as well as disappointment, sadness and conflict resolution.

By three or four years old, your child will really get into what I like to call creative play, where they are using their imaginations and story-telling abilities to create play scenarios that involve their new friend. The play is more complex and descriptive and they start really learning a lot about interacting with another child. They may run out with their friend and perform a show for you. They discover the act of sharing and how it can benefit them while considering the other child's feelings in the process. They learn the importance of taking turns and problem solving, especially when the parents avoid interfering and just let the kids play on their own.

Once children begin to socialize, it offers you the opportunity to socialize with your friends as well. Since many adult friends become parents approximately at the same time, it is very natural for your child's socialization to come from the children of your friends. As a reminder though, do not assume that your child will automatically get along with your friend's children simply because you are friends with their parents. Toddlers who are first introduced to the world of social play may very well act shy until they become comfortable with these strangers and the new environment they have been placed in. Be patient and let your child gradually connect with the other child without forcing them on each other.

A good way to do this is by offering both of them food and having each in a highchair, where they can be together, but separate. They can see each other, but don't feel like they need to actually interact with each other. By just sitting at the table together and eating without feeling threatened, they will gradually be able to watch the other child, hear them and see some of the amusing things they do. They may even start to mimic them. Once they seem more comfortable with this new friend of theirs, (and this may or may not happen on the first play date), you can sit them on the floor together and see what happens.

Other ways to get your child to learn and start feeling comfortable with another similarly aged child, is to sign up for a Mom's group, a fun class or spend an afternoon at the park. If this is your child's first experience with having a social life and you decide to sign up for a class, try to choose a Mommy & Me class for two and under. By attending a class with your child, their comfort level increases, and they will be more apt to participate and make the most of the class without feeling overly cautious and alone.

When you first introduce your child to another child that they don't know, do it in a very relaxed, casual atmosphere that gives your child the chance to adjust at their own speed and not yours. After a while, your child will begin to feel confident and safe and start venturing out in new ways as they express an interest in their newfound friend.

Play, whether it is individual, or social, (with a friend, you or a caregiver), is a huge step in your child's growth and development. Although a lot can be learned from playing on their own, (and this will continue as they grow), there are huge benefits from also learning what it's like to interact with someone their own age. Go ahead, play, have fun, run around, get some exercise and enjoy the smile on your child's face as they discover how fun it is to have a new friend.

Twenty One

BUILDING CHARACTER: FIVE IMPORTANT LIFE HACKS TO TEACH YOUR CHILD

Often in parenting, we tell our child to do things that we ourselves are not willing to do. Honestly, this will never work with children. Your child is watching your every move, mimicking what you say, how you say it and how you live your life. If you do it, they eventually will too, regardless if it is good or bad. You, at this point in their lives, are their most influential role model.

With that said, here are five life tips that you need to take to heart, demonstrate and pass on to your child. These are all key ingredients that go into building a person of character and what will be part of the mold as they become miraculous adults.

1. INTEGRITY

A person of integrity is someone who means what they say and says what they mean. They act according to their morals and their beliefs. For example, let's say your child is at a party with you and they are being aggravating. After a while of trying to encourage them to stop, you say:

For example, let's say your child is at a party with you and they are aggravating you for whatever reason. After a while of trying to encourage them to stop, you say, "If you don't stop, we are leaving this party." Then after you state that, the behavior still continues. At this point you have two choices (with only one of them being the one that a person of integrity performs). See if you can choose which one that is.

Option 1: You continue to state the same threat over and over to try to tame the attitude to no avail, but you never leave and if the truth be told, you never plan on leaving.

Option 2: The behavior continues so you get your coat, your child's coat, you walk out the door and leave.

Pretty simple choice, but yes, Option 2 is the one that shows integrity. You told your child what would happen if the behavior did not stop and it actually happened. This was not an idle threat, you followed through. You showed integrity and, in the meantime, you taught your child that you mean what you say.

When a parent never follows through with a threat, the child learns that they can behave however they want to behave, because nothing will ever happen. There will be no consequence. Your child will catch on to this "idle threat" thing pretty quickly. Remember, don't say anything that you don't mean and that you have no intention of following through with. If you say it, mean it and do it.

2. DON'T ASSUME

It is quite natural when we don't know something, to make an assumption. When we assume… well, you know the old adage, but in reality we add our own thoughts and feelings into a situation where our contributions don't belong. When you assume you are guessing about what someone else is feeling about a certain situation.

The key to remember is that none of us are mind readers; not you, not your partner, and especially not your child. To assume that someone else knows what you are thinking or that you know what they are thinking is preposterous. When you assume, you will never know the truth.

Teach your child these 2 rules of thumb:

a. The only way you will know what someone else is thinking is to ask them.

b. The only way someone else will know what you are thinking is to tell them.

"Questions are the gateway to conversation."
~ Celia Kibler

3. DON'T TAKE IT PERSONALLY

This one is hugely important to remember as we go through life. It is as important for you when parenting your child, as it is to teach them as they approach people and events that happen to them as they continue to grow.

This is difficult to understand and difficult to apply. When someone says something negative about you, it is important that you teach your child, that the comment is the problem of the speaker, not the receiver. What they have to say about you or a situation you are involved with, has everything to do with what is going on with them and actually nothing to do with you. They are using you as a vehicle to express their thoughts. Their thoughts are their thoughts and yours are yours and you can in no way control someone else's thoughts.

This is also true as a parent. When your child does something or says something that goes against your request, it is not about you. It is about something that is going on with them. Maybe they're tired or hungry, maybe they're testing their independence, maybe they're frustrated, maybe they are just in the mood to let it all out and scream. It's about them, not you. The part that's about you, is how you choose to respond to them. Your job is to help them understand what is going on, help them to recognize the feelings they are having and help them learn how to deal with those feelings in a calmer, more productive way.

When a child throws a tantrum or talks back, it is not about you at all, it is totally about them. So many factors play an important role in the tantrum or back talk. What's going on with them at that moment? Some factors that may cause a reaction like a tantrum or back talk; their age, their inability to explain themselves through speech, their inability to regulate their emotions due to their underdeveloped brain, their limited experience with the world in which they live, frustration, overwhelm, testing their boundaries, so many factors can play into their tantrum, Not one of their reasons for having a tantrum, is just to make you mad.

In fact, when you don't respond to their behavior defensively, and instead respond pro-actively and instructively, you are inadvertently teaching them that others' actions are not a reflection on them, but merely a reflection of the thoughts or feelings of the person expressing them.

4. ALWAYS DO YOUR BEST

This simple concept will take your child from childhood through adulthood with the ability to conquer anything. When you teach your child to always do their best and when they see you striving to do your best, the outcome of the activity becomes unimportant, because the focus is on the effort put forth.

Encouraging your child to do their best, teaches them to take pride in a job well done and to stop focusing on the outcome. Why is this necessary? Because the result can always be changed through implementing a different path or strategy. If the outcome is something that was not desired, then what is needed is to think of a new way of creating that result? Doing your best is what a person that works hard and consistently will do. This belief will eventually form a strong work ethic in your child and stay with them throughout adulthood.

Here's a common example: In school, parents are often so stressed about their children getting A's. When the entire focus of a parent is that a child must bring home an A, that child will get an A any way they can because they are striving to make their parents proud of them. Kids may resort to cheating or another dishonest form of achieving that grade because the total focus of their parents is on their grade. If they can't achieve that A, no matter what they do, they will begin to feel badly about themselves, think they are dumb, lose confidence and self-respect.

When we don't do our best, we accept lower standards for ourselves. We allow ourselves to make excuses, incorporate little effort, sacrifice neatness and continue through life with little heart and very little passion. We develop a negative view and disregard the positive.

Instead, let's turn it around and start focusing on their hard work and recognizing their effort. Start letting them know you see the effort they're making and the hard work they have done. At this point, their grades take a back seat to the way they've completed their assignment. This lets a child know that as long as they are doing their best, the result will be whatever the result turns out to be. If they want a different outcome, then strategize a different way of getting there, but continue to encourage your child to always do their best.

Just a heads up to remember as a parent. Recognize, that doing your best is based on many factors. If you are not feeling well, your best may be different than on a day when you are feeling at your optimum. If there are outside stressors going on, those things will also affect your ability to do your best. The same is true for your child.

In conclusion, be observant, be diligent in helping your child and focus on the effort. They will learn that what is important, is striving to always do their best in any situation. This behavior will give them the character trait of excellence, instill confidence as well as high self-esteem and they will grow taking pride in their work and in themselves.

"If a man is called to be a street sweeper, he should sweep streets even as Michelangelo painted or Beethoven played music or Shakespeare wrote poetry. He should sweep streets so well that all the hosts of heaven and earth will pause to say, here lived a great street sweeper who did his job well." ~ Rev. Martin Luther King Jr.

5. WE ALL MAKE MISTAKES

Mistakes are never to be feared. Mistakes are to be welcomed because without mistakes there is no learning, there is no growth, there is no success.

> *"Have fun making mistakes!"*
> ~ Celia Kibler

Mistakes should never be punished. Mistakes should be discussed, reviewed, interpreted, revised and developed into something that you were aiming for in the first place.

Often a misintention becomes a success, as in the case of the removable glue on a Post-It® Note. During the creation of one thing, another thing is discovered, like in the case of Play-Doh®, that was originally invented to be a wallpaper cleaner.

Thomas Edison experienced what some would say was 1,000 mistakes during his creation of the lightbulb. But when asked about all the mistakes he had made, he stated that in fact they were not mistakes at all, it just took him 1,000 steps to create the light bulb.

So where would those things be without the mistakes that brought them to life?

Mistakes and disappointments are merely speed bumps on the road to success. It's a time to pause, reflect, rethink and chart a new course. Celebrate the mistakes with your child, tell them about mistakes that you have made and teach them the resiliency that they will need as they experience life.

Twenty Two

SCHOOLS & DAY CARES: SEPARATING FROM YOUR CHILD

It's that time of year and that time in your child's life that they will be going to a school or starting a day care. There are two things at play here, how they feel and how you feel.

Answer a few questions for me please.

Are you afraid for your child? Are you worried they won't like it? Are you worried they will cry? Do you think you are more worried about this new experience or do you think they are?

One important step is to prepare your child for their new experience.

Here's some tips on how to do this.

1. Take them to the school or day care for a visit and a tour and a chance to meet their teachers/caretakers.

2. Talk to the school/daycare and see if you can attend at a time when your child can participate in a fun activity.

3. Allow your child to help assemble and choose whatever they will need for their school. Ex: backpack, lunch box, supplies, favorite doll or toy, etc.

4. Be honest and forthcoming to your child about what they can expect when they attend school. Who will be there, what will they be doing (activities, eating, napping, games, etc.)?

5. Be informed about how the new school/daycare is run. What kind of schedule do they keep and is it similar to your schedule at home? When is mealtime, naptime, etc.? Do you need to alter anything in your daily schedule at home so it more closely matches what your child will be doing in their new environment? Maybe at home your child eats at 12:30 and sleeps at 2, but at school they eat at 11:45 and sleep at 1. I recommend you begin altering your home schedule to more closely match the school's routine so that it is about the same regardless of where your child is.

   For example: My Grandson (3 years) naps at his school at 12:30pm. When in my care I would put him to bed at about 1:30pm. Once I realized the school nap time was at 12:30, I shifted his naptime to 12:45pm and it works well for him due to the consistency.

When your child is at their new daycare/school…

6. Nap Time… If your child does not sleep out of the home a lot, you may want to make sure he takes a special stuffed animal or even a shirt that may smell like you or his favorite blanket.

7. Transitioning... If this is your child's first experience with being out of the home for a full day, ask if you can start with half days at first so it gives your child an opportunity to adjust to their new environment. Then after a few days you can add an hour on each day until the full day is attended. If your child is adjusting well, you can move faster with the regular schedule.

8. Saying Goodbye... I hear a lot of parents tell me they just want to sneak out, so their child doesn't cry. Please do not do this. Your child needs to learn that sometimes Mommy or Daddy leave but they always come back. When you say goodbye to your child and tell them you will be back soon, the first few times they may cry and feel uneasy, but if you don't do this consistently, they will never feel confident when you leave them. In addition, they will never learn that when you say goodbye, you always come back. The staff at the facility you have taken your child to, should be well versed in this behavior and how to help a child move past their separation anxiety. In my over 35 years of experience having toddlers dropped off at my camps, a child who cries when their parent leaves is usually over it and participating within 2-5 minutes at the most. Be confident with the school/day care that you chose and know that they will help your child adjust to their new surroundings. Say goodbye, keep it short and sweet, a kiss, a hug, I love you and go. No lingering, no peeking in to see if your child is okay or has stopped crying. In short, go and come back when the day is over. If there is a problem, the staff will contact you.

9. Provide pertinent information about your child. Be honest and forthright with any behavioral issues, allergies, speech or anything that will help your caretakers offer the best care possible for your child.

   For example: I have been in situations in my own drop-off programs that I have operated. At one of our toddler-aged camp programs, a parent was not truthful about some of the issues their child was having, and it caused a huge problem for us in the classroom. When his outbursts began, we were not prepared to handle them as they had turned violent. Fortunately, my staff was experienced in the care of children with various behavioral issues, so what could have been a disaster, was quickly brought under control. After speaking to the Mom, she hesitated to tell us of his strong aggressive behavior, but once she finally admitted it, we were able to provide the child with an aid so that everyone had the best experience possible, especially her child. Be honest with your staff, the more they know, the more successful your child's experience will be.

10. Ask if the center will send you an occasional update during the day by email or text with a photo of how your child is enjoying their day.

Before choosing your daycare/school…

11. Visit a variety of schools in your neighborhood.

12. Get recommendations from friends and parents that you trust.

13. Make sure the location is convenient to you.

14. Be aware of the ratio of staff to children.

15. If there are multiple classrooms, ask how the kids are divided into these rooms. Is it by age, gender or something different?

16. What is their discipline policy and is it in line with your beliefs?

17. Ask about the ratio of outdoor play, TV/electronic play, reading, learning, crafts, etc.

18. Find out who provides the meals for your child, you or the school? What is included in the meals that they provide for their children (breakfast, lunch, dinner, snacks)?

19. Are there any special activities that your child will participate in? Are you charged extra for them?

20. What is their sick child policy?

21. What is their policy on outdoor play during very hot days?

22. What is the experience of the staff?

23. Are staff FBI fingerprinted?

24. Does the school and staff have proper certifications, including staff training in CPR and First Aid?

25. What is their diaper changing and/or potty-training procedure?

26. Read reviews and ask for recommendations for schools/daycare through your social media sites.

27. Once you have narrowed down the daycare/school, reach out to parents that attend the daycare/school and see how they like it and how their children like it.

A NOTE ABOUT SEPARATION AND YOUR TODDLER

Your toddler's biggest fear in leaving you is that they have no way of knowing that you are coming back. To teach them that they can trust that you will be back when you say you will is by ALWAYS saying good-bye and letting them know that you will be back soon or after work (however you choose to put it). Remember that toddlers do not have a good grasp of time like adults do. They don't really know what an hour means or what it means if you say you'll be back at 3. Saying you'll be back soon or after work is just fine for your child. Then when you come back to get them, be excited to see them, show them some love and let them help you gather their things to go home. Once in the car, you can talk to them about their day as well as what you'll be doing when you get home.

Although a big adjustment, this is an exciting time for your child. It's a time of growth, independence, learning, making new friends and having fun. If you are anxious about it (and many parents are), try not to pass that stress off to your child. Be positive, encouraging, tell them what a great time they will have playing and making friends and how proud you are of them getting so big. Approach your anxiety by talking to your partner, other Moms or Dads, your parents or work with a coach to help you through the stages of life.

Just a reminder to help your mornings go smoother, prepare as much as you can the night before. Pick out clothes for the morning, make lunches, put together back packs and what you need for yourself for the morning. A little extra preparation at night, can go a long way to bringing calm to a normally hectic morning.

You're all growing up together, treasure every moment, enjoy the roller coaster because before you know it, in the blink of an eye, they'll be all grown up.

SECTION 4

BEHAVIOR & RESPONSIBILITY

Twenty Three

CONSISTENCY: THE KEY TO GOOD PARENTING & BREAKING HABITS

This is the golden ticket! This is key!

Your consistency in following through with scheduling, routines, consequences and behavior, will create a family atmosphere of cooperation and cohesiveness that you all desire.

Without consistency, everything fails.

BREAKING HABITS

f you are trying to break a habit, let's say the pacifier. You decide you are going to choose a day to take the pacifier away during daytime, and only allow your child to have it at bedtime. If that is your decision, then the day you start, that's it. You do not give your child their pacifier at any time unless they're in bed. If they get fussy and you or the other parent or caretaker decide, "Well, just this one time. I really need to get this work done." Then, you go ahead and let them have it just this once, that's it. You now need to start over again because your child just realized that all they have to do is get fussy and you will give in to them and give them the pacifier. Whereas, had your child gotten fussy and instead of giving them their pacifier, you redirected them and started playing with bubbles or some balls or trucks, or even offered a healthy snack and water, then your consistency shows your child that they no longer will they be having their pacifier during the daytime and only when they are sleeping. After a few days of this consistent training and understanding, they will no longer react to not having their pacifier and they eventually won't even ask for it.

Breaking habits or starting new habits are totally dependent on your consistency with changing the behavior. I'm not saying it's going to be easy, but it is a part of the natural progression of growing up. To help you, be sure to include the new habit that you are creating into your child's routine.

For example:
1. Potty Training... Part of their morning routine when they first get up, is to sit on the potty. Part of the bath time routine is they sit on the potty before getting into the bathtub and after they get out.

2. Stopping the pacifier in the daytime... Before getting out of bed have a basket or special spot that your child can place their pacifier until they get back into their bed. It could be something as simple as laying them under their pillow or on top of the pillow.

3. Moving into a big kid bed or out of your bed (if you co-sleep)... Part of their night time routine can be to change into their pajamas in their own room, fluff up their blankets, get their dolls in place and choose books to read that they lay on their new bed.

Wishy-washy behavior doesn't work when breaking habits!
You cannot decide to start something like changing from co-sleeping with you to sleeping in their own bed, and do it on alternate days or be wishy-washy with your decision. It will never work, and the outcome will not be achieved. You will result in confusing your child, causing them undue stress and creating a much fussier child. You can avoid that by choosing a specific date, switch them into their bed, maybe lie down with them for the first couple of days and then allow them to sleep on their own. That's how you form new habits, consistency and commitment.

You realize you can't do it:
If you create something that you cannot stay consistent with, change it, BEFORE you put it into place. However, if you do put something in place, that just doesn't seem to be working well, there is nothing wrong with sitting down with the family and coming up with new ideas of how to make it better and then trying out that revised solution. When your child contributes to a solution and their opinion is respected, they recognize their value in helping their family function better.

Celebrate the behavior you want.
If you are working towards a certain outcome and that outcome is reached, get ready to celebrate. Your consistent acknowledgement and excitement for your child when they start achieving the results you are looking for, will encourage them to repeat what they did to get your initial approval. This is how you encourage your child to continue the behavior and lock in the new habit. Eventually, this newly changed habit will become the norm and the celebration, acknowledgement and extra encouragement will not be necessary and you can start focusing on the next phase.

It's all about consistency and commitment. Without the repetition, your child will not learn what you are trying to teach them. Toddlers thrive on consistency, repetition and routine.

I know there are days when it is hard to stick to the plan, you really just want to quit. Don't do it! Decide to be intentional and stick to it, you'll be so glad you did. You will be rewarded in the not too far future by your child breaking the habit, starting a new preferred habit and gaining their confidence and independence. Simply stated, you'll be super proud of them and yourself!

"Trust is built with consistency."

~ Lincoln Chafee

CONSEQUENCES

(refer to chapter 26 to learn about creating consequences)

As you read the chapter on consequences, remember that when you put a consequence in place, it is key to be consistent with it every time it is needed. Nothing is learned when you only use a consequence sometimes.

You either decide to put the consequence in place when the behavior warrants it, or you don't.

Twenty Four

EMPOWERMENT & INDEPENDENCE: IT'S A MATTER OF CONTROL... THEIRS!

Did you know that basically there are two reasons that a child decides to act out aside from the triggers that we have already discussed? When all triggers are met and they choose to act out in a negative way (with siblings, friends or you), making the wrong choices and causing a disagreement or fight, it is most probably over one of two things. Those two things are attention and control.

The key to battling this need for attention is to offer your child your undivided attention at various intervals throughout the day, even if it's just for 10 minutes.

The key to solving the control issue with your toddler is to empower them. Empower them with independence. Empower them with cooperation and listening skills. Empower them with self-control. Empower them to know that they are a part of their upbringing and have some control over what goes on in their life.

Imagine for a minute that you are a person whose entire life is controlled by someone else. They tell you what to do, how to do it, when to do it, if you're doing right or wrong, and yell at you if you try and fail. How would you feel? Kind of like a caged animal, right? This is how your child feels, so it's no wonder they throw tantrums and fight back. You would too.

I know what you're thinking, well, "They're two or three, and I'm the boss of them. They're too little to make decisions on their own." Well, you are the boss of them. However, they are absolutely not too little to make some decisions on their own if given the chance. The magic of this is when a child is given the opportunity to make a few simple choices, like which pair of pants to wear, they feel empowered, respected, encouraged and most importantly, "big".

NEGOTIABLES & NON-NEGOTIABLES

This is the beauty of the first step to empowering your child. Knowing where you can negotiate and where you can't negotiate, is the key to increased cooperation with your toddler.

Here's where you start:

Make a list of all the non-negotiable decisions you can think of and then make a list of all the negotiable decisions you can think of.

Example 1:
Non-negotiable: You must brush your teeth.
Negotiable: Would you like to use the blue toothpaste or the pink toothpaste? Let your child choose which one.

Example 2:
Non-negotiable: You have to get dressed.

Negotiable: Would you like to wear the flower shirt or the shirt with the stripes on it? Again, let your child choose which one.

Let's get started with the tips you need to know before you start offering your child choices on all the negotiables.

1. Don't feel like your child needs to have choices for everything, totally not necessary. However, the more choices you can give your child, the more willing they will be to cooperate when they do not get a choice.

2. Limit choices to only 2 items. Toddlers will get overwhelmed if given more than 2 choices.

3. If "no" is not an option, don't offer it as one.

Example: An unacceptable option: Do you want to go to bed now? The only answers to this question is YES or NO. If your child says NO and it is their bedtime, then what? You asked and you got your answer. So now what are you going to do? In fact, if you give them an option that is not acceptable and they choose that option, then you go back and say sorry, you have to go to bed. You are in fact doing more damage than good. When you give your child a choice, then they choose and you override that choice, you are sending them a direct message that their opinion doesn't matter. So be sure to only give choices where both options are acceptable.

An acceptable option: "Let's get ready for bed. Would you like to wear your dinosaur pajamas or your train pajamas?" Another acceptable option, "Would you like to read one book or two books tonight?" The bedtime is not the option (that's a non-negotiable); the pajamas are an option (that's a negotiable).

When a child feels that their world is partly their responsibility, even as a toddler, they feel like their opinions are valued, they are respected and in control of their life and not always at the mercy of someone else. They begin to understand that this family thing is teamwork and they're one of the players. They start cooperating more, happily.

CONSEQUENCES
(refer to chapter 26 to learn about creating consequences)

Here's another area where you can build a lot more cooperation and start your child to think more before they act and start learning how to regulate their emotions.

It all has to do with consequences. Try this, instead of you always coming up with the consequence, start letting your child have an opinion on the topic.

One of my clients asked her 4-year-old child what should be done the next time he talked back to her. He said, "I should have a time out." Mom asked him how long and he said, "3 minutes." She told him that worked for her and they agreed on the consequence. The next time he talked back to her, he told his Mom he needed a time out before she even had to say anything, and he went to his room. After that, there were very few instances of him talking back to her, because he knew he was going to have a time out. He learned how to speak to his Mom respectfully, so that the result was not his own punishment that he put in place.

SCHEDULES & ROUTINES
(chapter 25 dives into this deeper)

This also works when setting up schedules and routines for your child. Get them involved in what should be a part of the schedule or routine. Help them create it with you and they will more likely to stick to it. If you're setting up a morning routine with your toddler, ask them to tell you what they need to do in the morning, put it into a list. Then ask them what they do first, then what is second and so on… then work together to create their morning routine.

Empowerment and cooperation are simply a matter of giving your child more ability to contribute and take control where they are able to take control. Allowing negotiable opportunities to be the times that you give your kids choices on which way to go. The result of giving control back to your child, creates an atmosphere of more listening, cooperation, and independence. It will also reward you with more smiles, less trials, more family harmony and a whole lot more fun. After all, isn't that what you became a parent for?

Twenty Five

MASTERING SCHEDULES & ROUTINES

What's the difference, you ask?

A SCHEDULE includes the commitments of the day or week. Events such as School & Day Care schedule, religious activities, work schedules and commitments, Doctor appointments, extra-curricular programs, family events, meals, leisure and recreational activities are all included. The one thing you don't want to forget to include is your travel time between activities. If you don't include the time it takes you to get there, your schedule will be thrown off and chaos will return.

A ROUTINE includes all the activities required for a segment of time during the day. For example, you will need to set up a morning routine, a bedtime routine, after school routines and maybe even mealtime routines. In your routines, you need to include items like, hygiene, chores, homework, meals, showers/baths, getting dressed/changing clothes, playtime, reading and even screen time (TV, video games and computer, if applicable), etc. Whatever activities are needed during different times of the day is what you include. Routines should be as detailed as possible. These routines are then included in your schedule as a routine. Do not include the specifics within that routine.

This is an example of a schedule:

6:30am	Wake-up & start morning routine
8:00am	Leave for school (Mom drives)
8:30am	School starts
3:30pm	Dad picks up from school
4:00pm	Karate
5:00pm	Mom home from work
5:30pm	Homework
6:00pm	Dinner
6:30pm	Playtime
7:00pm	Bedtime Routine
8:00pm	Lights out

Hopefully, you get the idea. If you have questions, post them in our Raising Happy Toddlers group at Beabetterparent.com

Schedules and routines help your child know what is expected of them in a day or week. In addition, they help adults and children work more efficiently, allow children to become more independent and keep everyone aware of the comings and goings of the family.

So WHY do this? Why set up a daily schedule?
Without schedules, you and your family will miss appointments and activities. No one will know who is coming and who is going. Drop offs and pickups may cause confusion because you have not designated who or how your child is getting from one place to the other. A schedule will keep you from flying by the seat of your pants

and causing undue stress and aggravation. Simply, when schedules are put into place, communication is improved, and everyone is on the same page. No more missed appointments, driving schedules are pre-arranged and everyone's day will run much smoother knowing where they need to be, at what time and how they're getting there.

Why set up routines? Because, simply put, toddlers thrive on routines. Without a routine in place your child will have more stress and anxiety. They will feel lost and confused. A lack of routine creates a chaotic atmosphere for a toddler and for you. Their behavior will be affected and due to their insecurity from not having routines, they may become more defiant and definitely more irritable. This kind of daily stress has been proven to also cause illness in children and slow their development. When toddlers live life through various routines that are implemented every day, they build their confidence and self-esteem. When they know what is coming next, it gives them the courage to try doing things on their own. Their security and comfort increase and stress and anxiety decrease. Toddlers will cooperate more as they master their routines and begin to take personal responsibility for themselves and the jobs that need to get done within the routine. Routines make your child more adaptable and more independent. Routines also help to eliminate power struggles due to the fact that your toddler already is in the habit of the routine and knows what is expected of him. You don't have to constantly ask them to do things like brushing their teeth or getting dressed, it's already a part of the routine that they have become masters of. All of this mastery, enhances their skills and independence, improves their cognitive and physical abilities and creates good habits in your child that will benefit them for years to come.

Will changing or altering a routine completely throw off your child? The beauty of routines is that on the occasion when they need to slip out of it a bit; maybe relatives come to visit or there is a late event; the repetitive routine that they have become used to, allows your child to slip easily into it again on the following day.

I am often told by parents that Schedules and Routines are just way too hard to stick to. The truth is the chaos in your life that causes a routine or a schedule to be thrown off, is the chaos that will be calmed when you start implementing schedules and routines correctly and consistently.

Here are three important tips when creating your schedules.

1. BE REALISTIC… allow for travel and delays in traffic
2. ADD TIME for the unexpected
3. DON'T OVERSCHEDULE YOU OR YOUR CHILD

Once created, POST SCHEDULES & ROUTINES where they are easily visible to all. If you have a toddler that cannot read yet, you can set up a routine by using pictures.

EX: If at 6:30am you get dressed; you can have a picture of clothing. If at 6:45am you brush your teeth, you can have a picture of a toothbrush, etc.

The most important thing is to not give up! What doesn't work one day, may just work itself out the next. If you find that the schedule or routine is too tight in a certain area, then adjust it and add some time in or rearrange what is needed.

Here's an example of a morning routine

6:30	Wake UP
6:35	Go Potty
6:40	Get dressed (with the clothes you laid out the night before)
6:50	Straighten bed and pickup toys and clothes and put away
7:00	Brush hair and teeth and wash face and hands
7:15	Eat Breakfast and put dishes in sink after eating
7:30	Playtime
8:00	Leave for school/day care

Notice that in this morning routine, the child is woken up early enough so that this routine can include some playtime before they leave for school or daycare. This little addition of down time will make leaving for school or daycare much less eventful and much more productive. As a bonus if you play with your child for at least 15 minutes during the morning, they will happily go off to school or day care because they have had important one-on-one time with you.

HOW TO GET STARTED

To get started setting up your schedule and your routines, sit down with your child and brainstorm on everything that needs to be done, as well as what you all do to get it done. If your child is under 2 and not talking, then do this with your significant other or even on your own. My daughter could have easily done this at 18 months, since she was fluent at the English language by then and understood a lot of concepts. With that said, don't underestimate your toddler. Regardless of their age, if they have a good grasp of their language, they can help you do this. Make lists with everyone's ideas and then you can break it down by person and their specific activity.

After the lists are made, talk about the order activities can go in and create your routine or schedule.

HELPFUL TIPS

If you're setting up an evening routine, don't forget to include everything you need to get ready for the morning. Ex: Picking out clothes for tomorrow. Putting together backpacks and briefcases. It's also handy to have a box or basket close to the front door that you can put your backpacks, briefcases, etc. in so they're easy to grab and go when you're ready to leave. Prepare lunches the night before and you can even prepare breakfast if necessary. Hard boiled eggs, cut up vegetables and fruit make great grab and go food for breakfast, snacks or anytime.

SUPPORTING DOCUMENTS

If you visit our website, www.beabetterparent.com, you will find a lot of valuable documents that compliment this book. One of them is to help you set up your schedules and routines. Head over to the website and print out the .pdf, "Creating Your Schedules & Routines". So, now is the time to get started calming down and organizing your life and the life of your family.

Twenty Six

BOUNDARIES: THE KEY TO HELPING YOUR CHILD FEEL SAFE, SECURE AND LOVED

Parents hear all the time that they need to set boundaries for their child, but many parents will ask me to tell them exactly what a boundary is and how are they set up.

A boundary is a set limit, an understanding, a non-negotiable and these limits go a long way to helping your child feel safe and secure in your home. Without this sense of security, your child will feel stressed from living in a constant state of chaos. This stress will cause irritability, aggression, moodiness and will leave your child believing that they are in charge, not you. And honestly, without these limits, they probably are. They will think that they can do whatever they want because you have no control over them. Without set boundaries, for the most part, they are correct. Read over Chapter 11, Who's In Charge Here.

Boundaries and consequences go hand in hand, and you should be pro-active in setting up the consequence if the boundary is not followed. Put these limits into place prior to the incident occurring, if at all possible. When your child chooses not to follow one of the imposed limits or boundaries, you and your child are already well aware of the consequence.

What is the best way for you to be pro-active and set up the boundaries for your child? Start by making a list of all the behaviors that you consider to be non-negotiable. Here are some examples:

1. the way everyone speaks to each other… kindness, manners, no cursing, no name calling;
2. putting on your seat belt when you get into a car;
3. holding hands whenever you cross a road;
4. no throwing objects, biting or hitting;
5. no throwing food;
6. wearing a helmet whenever you ride a bike or similar wheeled toy
7. brushing teeth morning and night.

You get the idea and I hope at this point, you understand.

Now you've set up a list of boundaries, how do you express to your child what behaviors are acceptable and which ones are not? First of all, you can be pro-active and hold a family meeting (Chapter 4) so that you can talk about what is expected and what is not.

For very young children, you may not even set up a boundary until a violation has occurred.

For example, possibly you did not make it clear that we don't throw food in this house. Then lo and behold, at the end of dinner, your child gets irritable and boom, food is thrown. This is your cue to set that boundary now and fast. Take your child's plate away and firmly tell them, "We do not throw our food. Food is for eating and now that you have thrown your food, your meal is done." Then take them down from the table." Repeat this action EVERY TIME food is thrown. Do not laugh, even if you find it cute. Never allow a behavior to occur after you have addressed it and told your child they can't do that. If you do, they will get confused and they won't know when it is appropriate to follow a boundary and when it's not. The boundary becomes negotiable and then is no longer a limit or boundary. Stay consistent with following through on directions and consequences and your child will learn to stay consistent with eliminating the behavior that is not wanted and learning to make good choices.

Your tone and words matter when setting boundaries. You should be firm but not yelling. You should be direct and use age-appropriate language that your child understands. The simpler and more direct the instruction is, the better your child will follow through. Don't add words that are not clear. For example don't say "I don't think throwing your food is a good idea"… you don't think? Try this instead, "You cannot throw your food." The end, direct and to the point. Don't end a direction with the question "OK?" Do they have a say in this boundary? NO. This is non-negotiable and this must be followed. Whatever non-verbal cues you are using, as well as facial expressions should be in line with the firmness of your voice. When your words, tone of voice and non-verbal cues are in alignment, you will be taken seriously by your child.

Remember, a boundary or limit is not put into place to be mean to your child or to make their life harder. In fact, it's the complete opposite. In life, we have boundaries that we all must follow or there will be consequences. If you speed when driving, you run the risk of getting stopped by the police and given the appropriate consequence:

a ticket. Setting up boundaries in your child's life is the way you show them that there has to be a certain number of rules that everyone follows. When you choose to make a decision about whether to follow a boundary or not, you also choose to accept the consequence that results based on your decision. Welcome to life. Your child will be happier with boundaries, feel safer and more in control, while being able to live more comfortably in your home.

Twenty seven

CONSEQUENCES: THE RESULT OF CHOICE

*"You may not know what your child will do,
but your child should always know what you will do."*
- (author unknown)

As adults, we know that when we make a decision or a choice, it will have a result or a consequence that is determined by the choice we made. We start learning this as kids through the results of our actions and the consequences that our parents imposed on us. Make one choice you may have a great result; make another choice and you may have a result that you don't prefer. Whatever the outcome, it is based on the decision you made at the time.

All children need to learn that there are consequences for their actions, good or bad. Just like when toddlers react with full emotions and lash out at someone or something, they may find themselves in a time-out or reprimanded in some way. Decisions are followed up with results and we begin to learn this as children and continue using that knowledge as we grow up into adulthood.

As adults, we learn to think before we act. However, a toddler does not have that luxury. Yes, they can think and yes, they can act. However, their brains do not have the ability to put those two together and actually think before they act. Your child is unable, due to their underdeveloped brains, to make a reasonable decision based on logic or self-regulation and react calmly and constructively to a situation. Their reaction to an issue is just that a reaction, it is not thought out and it is not done on purpose. It is simply a reaction to an emotion. If they're mad about something they may yell, scream, hit or throw a tantrum. Whatever the reaction is, it is not within their power to control it… yet. That is where you come in as a parent or caregiver, to teach them how to regulate their reactions to their emotions.

Through consequences and conversation, we teach our children to understand their emotions, recognize when they show up and think about how to act in response to that emotion.

Here's a good place to start when you consider consequences for your child's actions. Begin by thinking about and writing down the emotional reactions that you have seen coming from your child. Then start working with the other parent, if applicable, as to what a proper response should be the next time your child handles that emotion in a negative way.

For example: Your child throws food at the table. What will be your response to your child throwing food? Maybe, you decided that when this happens, you take their meal away (which by the way is the response I suggest you use). Now you calmly say, "You are throwing your food, that must mean you are done eating. I am taking your plate away and you can get down from the table."

Be careful not to stifle the emotion that your child presents. Avoid saying things like, "If you don't stop crying, I'll give you a reason to cry." This indicates that they are crying just to cry, and although you may think that, a toddler cries for a reason. It may not be a reason you agree with (for instance saying "no" to something), but the disappointment that your child feels and that has caused them to cry, is still a very real emotion that needs to be addressed. How you react to the situation will help your child learn to deal with disappointment constructively. Learning how to deal with disappointment and other emotions is necessary for them to grow with emotional maturity through life. So just saying "Stop crying", is not offering any options of what they should be doing instead. Understand? Your job is to teach, explain, create and give examples for them to understand what all of these emotions running through their brain are about. Help your child learn to live with their emotions, regulate them, and grow from their experiences.

Why do they need a consequence?

Because every decision that every living thing makes, results in a consequence, whether good or not so good.

For example: You have been working on using manners with your child. Scenario 1: He asks for something and does not use manners. Your response may be, "Please try that again with your magic words." OR Your child does use their manners and they score a point on the Manners Board. (check out beabetterparent.com for directions on how to make your Manners Board).

A consequence should be one that helps them learn a lesson that they can then put into action at a later date. A consequence, although it may seem like a punishment, is in reality a way of teaching them that when you make a choice, an action or behavior is the result. When they choose to act in a negative way, the consequence encourages them to choose a preferred behavior the next time the opportunity presents itself.

Simply put there is a cause and there is an effect. There is an action and there is a reaction, a consequence. Although, people often refer to a consequence as negative, it isn't really, nor should it be. It can be quite positive. For example, your child ate all his dinner and as a consequence he gets to play a game after. Using it as a response to a negative situation will go something like this, your child threw his food and as a consequence he was removed from the dinner table.

What you should be doing is giving them a chance to calm down, while you calm down. Then discuss what happened and how you can come up with a more rational solution. Toddlers have to learn self-regulation, they are not born with it and that is where you as a parent come in to play.

STEP 1: When you are setting up consequences for your child, there are the 3 important elements that should always be considered when creating a successful consequence.

1. It has to RELATE. Let the punishment fit the crime.

> **For example** : You told your child, "Dinner will be ready in 10 minutes. I am setting a timer and when the timer beeps, you have to turn off your tablet and come eat." The timer goes off and your child does not turn off their tablet.

A proper consequence that relates to what occurred: The tablet is turned off and put away until tomorrow afternoon. Then you tell your child, "We will try again tomorrow, if you still don't turn off your tablet when the timer goes off, then I will take it away again." When you stay consistent with this consequence, in a couple of days, your child will learn that you mean what you say and they will turn the tablet off themselves, when the timer goes off. Success!

An improper consequence for this same behavior would be more like this. "I am taking your tablet away and you cannot have it back for a week." The problem with this overly long, extended punishment is that there is no opportunity to learn the positive behavior that you are trying to teach your child.

2. It must be REALISTIC.

Using the same example: You told your child, "Dinner will be ready in 10 minutes. I am setting a timer and when the timer beeps, you have to turn off your tablet and come eat." The timer goes off and your child does not turn off their tablet.

An unrealistic consequence would be you saying, "If you don't turn that tablet off, I will throw it away and you won't have a tablet ever again." Why is this unrealistic? Just ask yourself, are you really going to throw that expensive tablet in the trash? I doubt it (if you are, then fine, however I will tell you that this consequence is extreme and will not teach or resolve anything other than your child now has no tablet). They will not learn to understand what you are trying to teach them. All they will learn is that they have no tablet.

Do not make a consequence that you are not absolutely sure you are going to follow through with.

3. It must EDUCATE.

This one is the whole point of a consequence.

For example... as we said in number one, the consequence we came up with, will eventually teach your toddler how and why they should make a certain choice and what the result of that choice will be. They will learn to think before they act, because they will know what will result in their decision. Thinking before they act is the goal of all of this. It will ultimately teach your child to make a more informed choice.

STEP 2: What must you do when offering up the consequence.

1. Always be firm and consistent with your consequence. Once you have decided what the consequence is, you must always use it in relationship to that behavior. The consequence must always be your response until your child has learned to make the more cooperative choice. Express your pleasure and excitement for your child's ability to listen and cooperate.

2. If you don't mean it, don't threaten it!
What you threaten as a consequence, you have to follow through with. If you have no intention of following through, then don't say it, it will just become an idle threat.

For example: You are at a party that you want to be at, and your child is acting up and you tell them you will be leaving if they don't stop. When they don't stop, you HAVE TO LEAVE. If you don't leave, they will learn to never believe your threats and will learn that you are just bluffing. Your child will learn that they can continue to do whatever they want, because nothing will ever happen to them. You will lose all authority over your child and they will feel free to act however they choose.

3. Be on the same page.
What you say, goes for the other parent. If the two of you disagree, your child will play one against the other until they get their way. Remember, your child is not stupid and will eventually figure out how to get the results they want.

NOW IT'S YOUR TURN TO TRY

Question 1: What is a behavior of your child that you are trying to change?

Practice: Create a Consequence and follow through with it consistently until the behavior changes, regardless of how hard it is. If it doesn't work well the first time, don't give up!

Question 2: How did it work out? How difficult was it for you?

Twenty Eight

INSTANT GRATIFICATION VS. DELAYED GRATIFICATION

First off, let's analyze how you interact with your child. Are you giving in to them with every whine and every demand? Do you give in every time they say, "I want this"? Do you just hand them what they want to keep them quiet, without regard of whether they should have it at this time or even have it at all?

Let's think for a minute, think about all the candy that kids are offered just to keep them quiet. For example, you want to set limits on their screen time, yet they have been screaming and fighting and you say, "Here, watch your tablet and stop fighting." What just happened in this example, was that your child was just rewarded with something you were trying to limit, at a time when they should have been learning self-control. Next time they want something, they will know that if they fight or throw a tantrum, or create enough chaos to set you off, they will ultimately get what they want. Basically, instead of being pro-active with a situation, we act on emotion and stress and then regret the decision we've made. I know you have done this, because we have all done this at one time or another. This is not to make you feel even guilty, this is presented to help you recognize the times when we just simply give in without thought. These times are the hardest, but most important times to stick to the plan.

When you give in, you are creating a need for instant gratification. Basically, you are teaching your child how to behave, so that they get what they want immediately. Yes, I know sometimes it is easier, but is it worth it in the long run?

What does instant gratification teach your child? Instant gratification creates a moody, irrational child that will go to desperate means until they get what they want. The become entitled adults that no one particularly likes to be around. Is that really the kind of adult you want to raise?

Here are the behaviors that are instilled in your child due to giving in and teaching them that they must have immediate gratification.

- Your child will become impatient. They learn that there is no reason to work hard to achieve something, because they will just get it regardless.
- Your child will become entitled and unappreciative.
- Your child will become over-emotional. They whine, they demand, they get frustrated, disrespectful and ungrateful. Why? Because you are allowing them to.
- In the long run, it will make your child very unhappy, because a child that always wants something now and not later, can never be satisfied and therefore is destined to always be miserable.
- Your child will take things for granted. If they are given something immediately on demand, it loses its value almost as quickly.

- Decision making and problem solving is never learned and therefore creates issues for your child as they continue through life.
- They live with a ME FIRST ATTITUDE.

So, how do you change? How do you start giving your child the gift, and it is a gift, of DELAYED GRATIFICATION?

Stop giving in to their every request. You are not doing your child any favors. Start setting boundaries. If you are in a store and they throw a fit because they want a toy, you need to remove them and tell them something similar to, "At this time we are not here to get you a toy. If that is something you really want, we can add that toy to your gift list or savings list to buy at another time." We will discuss these lists and how they can teach your child when we discuss Allowance in this chapter.

Here's a big one. Are you modeling self-control? Do you spend every penny you earn? Do you have a savings account? Do you talk to your child about the things that you want and discuss what you will need to do in order to obtain it? You need to not just talk the talk, but walk the walk. When your child sees you working towards a goal and waiting until it's earned, they learn self-regulation. They begin to understand what it feels like to actually wait for something until they are able to go through the steps needed to achieve it.

Start practicing GRATITUDE every day. Begin a gratitude journal, for you and your child. You can even start a family journal, where everyone writes in the same journal each morning and evening. The daily practice of gratitude has been proven to create people that are more appreciative and happier. Gratitude creates children that are less demanding and far more content and happy with their life as it is.

Start working on family projects that require a wait time. For example, starting a family vegetable garden, where everyone (even the youngest child) can get involved digging, and tilling. Planting is a great way to spend quality time while creating something that requires everyone to be patient as they watch and get excited about what is growing. A vegetable garden offers the additional benefit of allowing your child to eat their harvest right out of their garden. It's a great way to get your child to eat more vegetables and a great way to teach delayed gratification. Be sure to share in our group (tamingthetoddler.com) what projects you and your child are working on, that are teaching them delayed gratification.

Start teaching your child about Money Management. Just in case you were wondering, it is never too late to teach this. Talk about budgeting and what it costs to run your household (rent/mortgage, electricity, water, food, clothing, medical, savings, etc.). When you teach your child money skills, you are setting them up for a lifetime of financial success and understanding the difference between desires and needs. You can start doing this through allowance. Your child's allowance should be offered strictly to teach money management. Their allowance should not be connected to their weekly household chores, as those are required responsibilities of everyone in the family. You can however, offer your child to work on jobs and chores that go above their usual weekly requirements. These extra jobs allow them to earn more money for specific items that they want. This also teaches the importance of working hard for what you want. When we give into our child's every desire without teaching this, they learn that if they want something, they get it, even if no effort was exerted at all. Set up separate categories for their allowance. One is for what they need NOW, a second is what they want to SAVE FOR, a third is for CHARITY. They can always have a wish list for special occasion gifts that people are looking to buy for them. This wish list will not impact their personal money.

SAVINGS: The amount that they put into a savings account should be a percentage of their allowance. A suggestion would be that 10% goes into savings. The savings could be placed in a piggy bank or an actual bank savings account (this also gives the opportunity to teach and demonstrate for your child the difficult concept of compound interest). If they have things on their "SAVE FOR" list and if they want to earn it faster, they can opt to take a higher percentage of their allowance to add more to their savings account. They can also opt to do additional household chores to earn more money above their regular allowance.

Example: My son is a video gamer and always has been. He ultimately received his bachelor's degree in Video gaming and has been working in the industry ever since. When he was growing up, he always wanted the latest and greatest game console that was on the market. We talked about how game consoles were expensive and although I would be happy to buy him games for birthday and holiday gifts, I would not buy the consoles. If he wanted more consoles than the one he already had, he would have to save his money to buy them. He decided that was what he wanted most and became a master at saving his money--asking for donations to his "game console fund" at gift time, and doing extra chores to earn extra money. He was eventually able to buy all of the consoles he wanted, using all of his own money. This taught him how great it felt to actually work for what he wanted, as opposed to just being given everything without effort. As a bonus, it was an ideal way to teach him delayed gratification. At no time was he ridiculed or judged for wanting these things. He was only taught that if this is what he wanted, it would require work and money management to get there.

When your child asks for something that you are not willing to buy for them, ask them if they want it badly enough to save for it. If the answer is yes, then it goes on their SAVE FOR list and you can sit down with them and map out what they will need to obtain it.

Including CHARITY in their allowance categories, teaches compassion and goes along with learning gratitude and understanding that there are others that are less fortunate than they are.

All kids need to have responsibilities. Responsibilities very often take priority over other activities that your child wants to do.
For example, your child wants to go out and play but he was supposed to pick up his toys an hour ago. Make it clear to him, that picking up his toys will be first and then he can go out and play.
Your child needs to learn priorities and not allowing them to skip responsibilities that you have in place, will teach this. Schedules and routines also help with keeping your toddler on task and understanding that everything will happen in due time as they go about their day.

Learning the value of delayed gratification will serve them well through everything they do throughout their life. It will also instill in your child a strong work ethic and a respect for themselves and others.

Twenty Nine

CHORES: MAKING THEM FUN FOR EVERYONE, EVEN TODDLERS

People often ask me, "At what age should my child start doing chores?" My answer, as soon as they can walk well, balance and hold something.

Children naturally want to help their parents, so let them. When your child becomes curious about how you load the dishwasher, that's your moment to ask, "Would you like to help?" Even a small child can put in a plastic bowl or dish or a spoon or fork. They will be so excited that you asked them and will feel so accomplished when they actually do it. Remember not to criticize how they do it, just mention what a good job they did. You can always fix it after they leave.

There are so many benefits to helping around the house. First off, your child learns to become something bigger than themselves. They become a contributing part of your family. Secondly, chores teach responsibility and the realization that there are things that must get done. When everyone pitches in, the jobs are finished quicker and everyone can move on to something else. Inadvertently, you are teaching your kids what it's like to possess a strong work ethic.

Children learn to cooperate and work together. More great qualities are gained like self-esteem and self-confidence and self-worth.

When creating chores for your child, remember their age and abilities. Don't give them a chore to do that is way above their ability to do it. Toddlers can do simple chores like dusting (spray a little of the cleaner on the table and give them a rag to wipe it off), vacuuming with a light-weight vacuum, sweeping, and cleaning windows.

What about their bedroom you ask? I recommend that you include straightening their bedroom as be part of their morning routine. Even your toddler who's in their own bed, can pull up covers and just smooth them out, put stuffed animals that fell on the floor back on the bed and pick up their clothes and put them in the hamper. Don't expect perfection, allow them the opportunity and time to try, learn and get better and better.

Be sure to stay focused on their effort, not their result. Your child wants to help out, they want to please you and do their best. However, if you criticize what they do and how they do it, you will smash their desire to help you, as well as their confidence and self-worth. It will also send the message that nothing they do is good enough for you. That thought will stay with them for a lifetime. So, if they are helping out, doing some kind of chore, feel free to demonstrate what you want them to do before they begin and how you do it. Once they begin, let them do it. If you feel there are places that have been missed (like spots on a table after dusting), don't criticize and say, "Oh you missed these spots." You can either grab a rag and offer to help them (but ask them first) OR go back and touch up the work they did AFTER THEY ARE DONE AND WHEN THEY ARE NOT IN THE ROOM. Don't ever touch up work they did in front of them.

Next question I am often asked is, "Should my child's allowance be tied to their completion of family chores?" I advise you to keep allowance separate from their regular household chores. This is the reason: Offering allowance is a way to teach your child money management. Family chores teaches your child that they are a part of this family and you all have a responsibility to work together and keep your home tidy and organized. Simply because a chaotic environment causes more chaos mentally for everyone. Chaos causes stress, stress causes distraction and disfunction.

So how do you teach your child that hard work and pay go hand in hand? If your child is working to earn some additional money for a goal they want, create chores that go above and beyond the usual household chores. When your child completes those chores, they earn additional money. For example, if they help put away groceries each time, they can earn extra money. If you have leaves to rake or gardening to do, that can earn extra money helping with that. If they wash your car, they can earn extra money. This should give you an idea of some ways to include them in additional work that needs to be done around your home (with the opportunity for them to earn more money).

Now let's get into some ways that you can make CHORES MORE FUN!

Remember, your child is much more likely to do stuff when it's fun. Be sure to go to the website (beabetterparent.com) that coincides with this book and pick up the .pdf of some great games and activities that can make family chore time a fun time.

GAMES YOU CAN PLAY to help out with the daily chores:

1. The Dice Game: Have every number of the dice indicate what chore needs to be done with a FREE DAY for one of the numbers. Example: 1=Dusting; 2=Vacuuming, etc.

2. The Sock Game: Put all the socks that have no matches in a pile, everyone picks up 5 socks and continue to play the game like you're playing the "Go Fish" card game.

3. The Meal Planning Game: Everybody can help plan meals. Get 4 Paper Lunch bags and label them Proteins, Vegetables, Fruit, Grains. Each member of the family has a piece of paper where they write 3 of their favorite foods for each category. Cut the foods apart and place each strip in the appropriate bag. Then each family member gets a turn to pick one food from each bag to create a meal. Keep going until all the food strips are used up and your meals are planned for the week. Write up your shopping list off of the meals created.

4. Busy Box: Great for when they tell you "I'm bored." When they get bored have them pick one thing from the busy box. Include all kinds of fun and household activities in this box and you will watch them start getting things done or at least not say "I'm Bored" so much.

5. Color Game Food Shopping: Each child chooses a color for when you go shopping. Have each child pick out a fruit and/or vegetable in the color of the day. Encourage them to choose food items that they have never tried before.

6. **Clean & Move:** Put on some fun loud music to clean by. You and the kids select cleaning stations. Every time you stop the music, each person has to move to a new cleaning station and start cleaning there. Put the music back on to energize then stop it again and move to the next spot.

Get your child to create new games to get things done. When you're having fun, everything becomes a game not a chore. Now stop reading and go get some stuff done!!

Thirty

"I'M BORED": THOSE DREADED WORDS & THE OVERUSE OF ELECTRONIC DEVICES

Does your child often come to you to say these two simple words, "I'm bored"? In this world of easily available electronic entertainment, our kids become very used to instant gratification and being entertained almost 24/7 by something other than themselves.

Allow me to remind you of something parents, "you are not responsible for your child's constant entertainment." Good news, huh?

Let's first address the many benefits of having "nothing to do".

The first is: down time allows for renewal, a restart. It allows your brain to have a break, which has been proven to improve brainpower and focus. Another benefit is that a lot of creative ideas and new concepts come from a place of quiet thought.

The key thing to remind your child is that the only person that can make them bored is themselves. Your child needs to find the delight in a variety of activities as well as the ability to come up with ideas of things they can do on their own.

If the answer to boredom is always a cell phone, tablet or TV, there are going to be some very problematic repercussions that happen.

THE PROBLEMS OF EXCESSIVE SCREEN TIME

1. Although giving a child their tablet is a very easy fix to, "I need to get some things done…", if your child is allowed to watch for too many hours a day, many problems arise.

What happens when your child learns to communicate through electronic speech?

First of all, a child that is just allowed to have endless screen time, especially a young child that is in the middle of language development, will be learning their speech electronically. This will cause future communication issues from their lack of conversation with actual humans.

Electronic speech does not enhance or encourage the expressive development of language skills. Communication is 60% non-verbal communication and only 40% the words we say. If your child is not consistently involved in conversation with you, their siblings or peers and instead are spending too much of their time isolated in front of an electronic device, many skills vital to communication & emotional development are never learned. Very often parents are barking commands at their kids from another room. They are not engaging their kids in conversation that can take on creative thought, expression and discussion. Humans model sentence structure, language enrichment and non-verbal cues. However receptive language, that is used when your child is watching a video game or utilizing an electronic learning program, is not all bad and does help children develop comprehension skills. What they are not developing, is the ability to read human facial expressions, body language and other natural communication cues like tone of voice. Since 60% of communication is non-verbal, it is a fact that you cannot develop interpersonal relationships, known as social communication, from a screen.

2. Excessive Screen time creates seclusion instead of encouraging social settings that allow a child to develop interpersonal relationships.

If your child is constantly secluded from the overuse of electronics, it can result in a lot of loneliness, self-centeredness, and a lack of caring for others' personal needs and desires. Focusing on a screen for a long period of time can contribute to obesity, vision issues and can affect long-term cognitive & emotional development. When everyone in the family is doing their own thing all of the time and everyone seems to be on their own screen, your child can lose their connection to your family and begin to feel lost.

3. So, what's a parent to do?

Let's come up with some great options to address the "I'm Bored" statement, that are alternatives to something with a screen.

    a. The Busy Box: Take a small cardboard box (shoe box or similar) and ask your child to write down, draw or tell you about activities that do not involve a screen. Encourage them to include anything they can think of. Examples: Reading, puzzles, cards, coloring, stickers, models, paper and markers to draw, modeling with clay, writing in a journal, playing outside, making a funny face, dance & sing, storytelling, etc.

These ideas are written down and cut into strips and placed in the Busy Box. When your child says that they are bored, you as their parent or caretaker, can hand them the box for them to choose an activity and solve the problem of boredom. Eventually, your child will reach for their Busy Box themselves, whenever they're looking for something to do.

b. The Fun Wheel: Take a large piece of cardboard and attach a pointer in the middle of the cardboard. Divide the board into sections so that when the spinner is spun it lands on one of the sections. Have your kids come up with what they want in each section, (things similar to activities in the Busy Box). Then spin the wheel, land on an activity, and the boredom problem is solved!

c. Go Fish Socks: A great way to solve the missing sock problem of life. Collect all the socks in a basket and gather around the basket with the kids. Everyone chooses 5 socks out of the pile and the game begins. Just like "Go Fish" the classic card game, each player holds up a sock to see if anyone has a match in their hand, if not, the player chooses a new sock out of the main sock pile. If it's a match, lay down the match, if not, it stays in the players hand and the next person continues the game. A fun way to get the socks matched up!

d. The Dice Game: A great game to get some chores done in the house. When your child complains they're bored, then it's a great time to play the Dice Game. Use a single die (unless you have so many chores, you want to use two), and make a chart (The Dice Game can be downloaded from beabetterparent. com or you can make your own). You can select any chores you want for this game, however, be sure to make them age appropriate. We will discuss this further in Chapter 28 where we talk specifically about chores. Then each person in the family (Parents can do this too) roll the die and then refer to the job chart as to the chore you will be expected to do. It's fun and it gets the job done.

The idea here is that if your child complains that they're bored, there are choices to give them something to do. As this continues in your family, your child will learn to come up with their own creative activities when they feel bored instead of coming to you.

SECTION 5

TRIALS & TRIBULATIONS

Thirty One

THE PICKY EATER: IS MAC & CHEESE YOUR ONLY OPTION?

Let me just start with something you probably don't want to hear. Are you a picky eater? Do you eat a variety of foods? Do you eat your vegetables, or do you make faces at them (not the kids, the vegetables)?

I've worked with a lot of parents over the last 30 some years and I have discovered that parents are always amazed at how picky their kids are about eating certain foods and when asked if they themselves eat those foods, they answer no! And more often than not, they don't even make them for their kids.

You can't expect a child to do something that you yourself are not willing to do.

For example, a parent was talking to me about her "picky eater", and the fact that her child would never eat vegetables. I was asking her if she ate vegetables and she said only salad. I asked her about broccoli and without thought, she made a gagging face and said, "No way!" --right in front of her son. I knew at that point, he would never eat broccoli when she was around. She decided for him and predetermined his taste for it, simply by making a single gesture.

Now in reality, kids have a lot more taste buds on their tongue than adults do. In addition, not everybody likes everything and that's perfectly ok. There is a lot of different food out there to discover. The idea is to offer your child a variety of foods that you are eating as well, without predetermining whether they will like it or not.

But what if you are not picky or judgmental, and you do eat a variety of foods, but you just can't get your child to eat them too? Here are some helpful tips that will encourage your child to start trying new foods and exploring their tastes a little more.

1. THREE NO-THANK YOU BITES!
When you offer your child a new food that they have never tried, make it a rule in your house for everyone (adults & kids) that you always take 3 no-thank you bites. They can be small (not miniscule) but you have to take 3 of them to determine if you really like or don't like a type of food. One is not enough. You may dislike the first and then love the second bite.

One day, I offered my Grandson some Roasted Seaweed Sheets and he said almost immediately, "Gamon (that's what they call me), is this going to be one of those foods that I don't like with the first bite, but I love on the second bite?" I said, "Absolutely!" He continued to eat the entire package.

When you make the 3-No-thank-you-bite rule the norm, they learn not to question it because they know in advance they have to at least try the new food.

2. ADD A MINI-BUFFET

When sitting down for a meal, add a little buffet in the middle of the table the contains food that complements the meal. For example grapes, blueberries, celery and carrot sticks, hummus, cherry tomatoes, chickpeas, beans, sliced sweet peppers, etc. Have this mini-buffet in the middle of the table, don't talk about it, just have it there. You can snack on it, others can snack on it and before you know everyone will complement their meal with a few fun treats from the buffet.

Bonus Tip... if you want your child to eat more vegetables and they're hungry before dinner is ready, let them sit down and start snacking on a buffet of veggies. If they're really hungry, they will eat them.

3. LET YOUR CHILD HELP PLAN, SHOP & PREPARE THE MEALS.

When your child gets involved in meal planning, shopping and cooking, they not only learn how fun it is, they also learn some new skills while you demonstrate how much you respect and rely on them. It's a win-win for everyone. You get help, they feel important and have fun! When your child is a part of the solution and contributes to the meal prep for the family, they tend to be much more willing to eat what they have made.

Taking your child shopping, is a great way to start teaching about nutrition, food labels and healthier options.

Bonus Tip: You can pretend your kitchen is a restaurant and you can get your child a little chef hat to wear and serve up the food to your guests (the rest of the family). Make it fun and the eating just might become secondary to all the good times.

4. BE CREATIVE

Let's get real, there are just some kids that no matter what you do, refuse to eat more than the 5 things they like. So, after you have tried all of the tips in this chapter, if you are still struggling, think of new ways to make their favorite foods. Be creative. Look up recipes by searching the specific food they like. For example, when I remarried, I gained 3 sons. One of my sons was a very picky eater and only liked about 3 basic things: Rice, Mac & Cheese and Chili. This was totally new to me, since my kids and I have always enjoyed a lot of variety in our meals. Now I was faced with the dilemma of having a child who had very strong opinions of what he would eat and what he would not eat. Of course, said child is now 35, so the internet was not like it is now and in fact, had really just began. So, I would search cookbooks for new varieties of these foods that the whole family could enjoy. We obviously didn't eat according to his tastes every night, but we would try to find options that might satisfy his simple palate, while satisfying everyone else. Therefore, my advice to you is that you try different ways to prepare their favorites. If they love bananas, search the internet for new and creative ways to serve bananas. If they love beans, search out new bean recipes. If you usually bake their favorites, try frying, grilling, blending, roasting. Being a creative cook won't just open doors for your picky eater, you may just find a favorite family meal that everyone loves.

Here are some more creative ideas that your child can help you make.

Want to add more vegetables or fruits to the diet?

Grind them up finely and add them to things like sauces, smoothies & salsa. Kids love food that they can prepare, so let them help you make a variety of toppings for baked potatoes and tacos.

Encourage your child to make their own trail mix. Go shopping, choose the ingredients (nuts, seeds, raisins, dried fruit, carob or chocolate chips, coconut, etc.), let them help you pick ingredients out and make their own trail mix. Trail mix is a healthy snack or can even be a quick meal.

Kids can even create their own pizza. (Look for a fun & healthy Kids meal that all of you can make at the end of this chapter).

5. BE THE EXAMPLE & DON'T PREDETERMINE WHAT YOUR CHILD WILL EAT

As I mentioned earlier, be the role model when eating food. Be willing to try new foods and eat a variety of food at each meal. Do not assume your child won't like a food offered to them before they have even had the chance to try it. Let them (and you) follow the "3 no-thank-you" bites rule.

6. DON'T BECOME A SHORT ORDER COOK

Make one meal for the family. Add the mini buffet mentioned in #2 if you would like. But do not cook a different meal for each person. This only caters to your child's refusal to eat what you have made. If your child knows that you are willing to make anything they want, they will refuse to eat anything you make. Don't give in. If they want to leave the table, let them leave. If they get hungry later, offer them their meal again, do not fix them something else until they have eaten what you originally prepared for them.

7. SERVING SIZE

Be sure to feed your child age-appropriate servings, they can always have more if they're still hungry. Here's the easy serving size gauge… for kids and adults. Your serving size for each part of your meal, should be the size of the person's fist that is eating. So, your fist size is for your food, your child's fist size is the size of each portion of the food on their plate. Part of the problem is that you are just giving your child way too much food to eat at one sitting.

8. EASY ACCESIBLE SNACKS

Make sure you fill your fridge with snacks that are easy to grab and healthy too. If your kids want a quick snack, they can go grab something healthy and easy out of the refrigerator.

If you have to run out quickly to go somewhere, have some grab n' go food available. You can put some veggies in a zip-lock bag to take with you. Boil up a dozen eggs, peel them for ease and put one or two in a bag that can go with you easily. Buy seeds, nuts and dried fruit and put them together as a trail mix that you can keep in your car. It's high energy, low cost, easily available and is not affected by the temperature changes in a car.

9. PLAY WITH YOUR FOOD

Food can be so fun. Eating with toothpicks, adding dips, cutting food into shapes (using cookie cutters), making fun faces on plates using a variety of healthy foods. Be creative and let your kids help make eating fun. Let them create their own silly face of food. Here are some great ingredients that you can use. Blueberries, apple slices, banana slices, peas, carrot slices, egg slices, celery sticks, broccoli for scenery, etc. Then eat the trees first, or the eyes, or the arms. In other words, make meal-time, fun time.

Great dips are hummus, salsa, salad dressings, yogurt, honey, and peanut butter...be creative and you just might be surprised at what your child will eat.

FAVORITE MEAL RECIPE TIME!

Does your child love pizza, soda and ice cream? Now you can make the Good-For-You Version. Here's how…

PIZZA:

Ingredients:
- Whole grain tortillas
- Low sodium Spaghetti Sauce
- Mozzarella and/or Cheddar Cheese

TOPPINGS:
- Ground Beef
- Chicken
- Lean Deli meats
- Pre-cooked Bacon/Sausage (grease fully drained)
- Broccoli
- Sweet Peppers
- Olives
- Tomatoes
- Onion
- Mushrooms
- Pineapple
- (or add what you love to it)

Let your kids make their own.

SODA: REPLACE SODA WITH A SPRITZER

In an average glass (whatever you use for you or your child)

Fill glass 1/3 of the way with your favorite 100% Fruit Juice

Fill the glass the rest of the way with sparkling water, seltzer or club soda.

Add some frozen fruit into the drink instead of ice

A Party drink Umbrella always makes it fun!

ICE CREAM: Make NICE CREAM instead.

1. Pre-freeze your over-ripe BANANAS (Be sure to peel the banana before freezing)

2. In a food processor add the banana, ½ cup of milk or alternative milk (almond, rice, cashew, coconut, etc.)

3. Blend it all up and you have a delicious bowl of super smooth tasty ice cream.

Add some fun...

You can add frozen fruit to the mix, nuts or seeds, honey or anything you like on ice cream.

BONUS MEAL HACKS:

If they don't want to eat...

      1. Take their plate of food & divide it in half and let them choose the half they want to eat.

      2. Serve on larger dinner plates so it looks like there is not as much food for them to eat.

      3. PLEASE NOTE: If they start throwing food, they are done. Don't discuss it, don't try to keep placing the food on their plate/tray and telling them you need to eat. When food is thrown, you tell them, "Well, I see you are done eating now" and take the food away and put them down. They will soon figure out that this is not a game and you mean business. Stay consistent with this technique and don't give in.

Thirty Two

SCREEN TIME ON YOUR TIME: HOW DO I GET MY CHILD OFF THEIR TABLET?

You are not alone. Let me tell you, in this day and age, parents everywhere are asking this same question. Tablets, video games, electronics are very addicting, we know that as adults, and as they become more and more available, kids are becoming addicted too.

Let's start with the negative effects of too much screen time. You may have noticed this already with your child, that when they are on screens too much, they lose interest in everything else. They just want to watch their screen. Their health becomes affected from poor eyesight to obesity from lack of movement, to sleep issues and extreme moodiness. In addition, there is a huge element of needing instant gratification and they begin to want everything now!

So, what's a parent to do? How can we get those kids to do other things rather than gluing their face to their favorite electronic entertainment?

YOU AS THE ROLE MODEL

First of all, let's discuss your use of your cell phone or other electronic devices. Do you always have a phone in your hand? Do you talk to your child while also looking at your phone? What does your screen time look like? Are you regulating your own time and creating a role model for your child to emulate? If you don't think you are, it would be advantageous for you to start analyzing your own screen time habits and begin changing your ways immediately. As I will remind you again and again, monkey see, monkey do.

Now let's chat for a minute about who's in charge here? Hint: You are!

You absolutely have the right to say when and where they get to use their screens. Screen time should always be considered a privilege not a requirement. You should already have a daily schedule and if you don't, create one now. I recommend after you read this chapter, stop and create your daily schedule (If you need some help, see Chapter 25 on Schedules & Routines). Incorporated in that daily schedule should be, yes, you guessed it... screen time. If there is a start and end time for screens included in your schedule, then everyone understands and stay on the same page.

Now, I know what you're thinking, "In theory, this sounds great, in the real world (my house), it ain't happening." Well, good news, it absolutely can happen if you stay consistent and create consequences.

So, let's start with the consequences. Remember that a consequence is created to teach your child, not punish them. It is established to teach a behavior that you want to develop and encourage with your child. The beauty of tablets, video game consoles, laptops, phones, etc.... is they're small and portable. A perfect characteristic for easy removal.

So, let's start with this scenario. If you give your child a time limit and they argue, fight, scream, throw a tantrum about stopping, pick the tablet or whatever they're having a fit about and take it away. Unplug it and move it. Do not give it back until the next day and explain to your child that we have an agreed time limit and when time is up, time is up. When you give it back to them the next day, remind them again. Set an alarm to remind them of when the time is up and then when it goes off, done. If they decide to argue again with you about stopping, repeat the action of taking it away and maybe this time skip a day before they get it back. The idea is that through your reminders and consistency and consequences, they will learn that you mean what you say and they will stick to the plan.

Consistency counts. You must be consistent in all aspects of parenting and life for that matter. If you want to reach a goal in your own life or with your child, consistency is key in making that happen. When you stay consistent with your child, you create an atmosphere of comfort for them. You provide them security--they know what to expect and they know you stand by your word. You directly teach them what it is to be a person of integrity. A quality that I wish more people had.

Offer options. Start encouraging and asking your child to create activities that you can do as a family. For example: game nights at home, puzzles, after dinner walks, going to your local playground or park, story time, tea-time. All of these activities encourage fun family engagement with one element missing, screens. Screens tend to divide us. When you are intentional with family activities, you are bringing your family together and creating a strong bond and a realization that you are all a part of something bigger than yourselves.

Create daily chores (Chapter 28) for everyone, including straightening their rooms, helping prepare meals and cleaning up. This instills responsibility and increases movement and family unity.

Lastly, have a family meeting (Chapter 4) and let everyone brainstorm about the limits that the family should have with their screens. Then make final decisions based on everyone's ideas and decide on when screens are allowed and when they are not. Toddlers can be a part of suggesting screenless events like mealtime and outdoor playtime with your encouragement and that will help them to feel that you take in interest in what they want. It gives them that little control over their life and will empower them to be more cooperative at other times during their day.

The bottom line is that you have final say, not your child. It is important for your child to have limited screen time, where you enforce the schedule and that you also model self-control on your devices too.

Thirty-Three

TATTLING VS. TELLING

Two kids are playing, things aren't going well. You're busy doing something else. All of the sudden, appearing out of nowhere, comes your child to whine to you about all the things the "other kid" did to them.

What is your response? Do you immediately take the side of your child? Do you immediately run to scold the other child?

OR...

Do you calmly see what's going on? Do you ask your child to speak to you in a nicer voice?
Do you wonder, "here he goes again, tattling! I wish I knew why he does this."?

If your response is the first scenario where you immediately take the side of your child, without finding out what is really going on, you are encouraging your child to tattle and they will tattle for a long time to come unless you change your ways and give them a chance to change theirs.

Just so you are aware, most children do not begin tattling until they're around 4 or 5 years old. The tips I am offering you are very age-appropriate for a child that chooses to tattle.

Before we start with the "Why" they tattle, let's address the difference between "tattling" and "telling". It's actually fairly simple although a parent may get confused. Let's start with Tattling.

"Tattling" is when a child comes to you with a problem about another child that presents no danger. The intent of tattling is to get someone else in trouble.

Example: Bobby runs to Mommy to tell her that Joey grabbed the toy that he wanted.

"Telling" is when a child comes to you concerning a dangerous or a potentially dangerous situation with the intention of helping someone else. Ex: Bobby runs to Mommy to tell her that his little brother Joey pulled a power cord from the wall.

First of all, let's address the why? Why do kids tattle? There may be a variety of reasons this happens. First of all, your child may be wanting some of your attention and they know they will get it if they run to you with a problem. Possibly a house rule was broken, and they feel it's their job to report it. Maybe they are looking to get their friend in trouble and show their friend a little of who's in charge here. Often, they want to change the rules and show how you are always on their side even if the spat is between siblings.

So what should you do about all these? How do you explain to a child that tattling is different than telling? You need your child to be aware and tell you about possible risky or dangerous situations.

Here's where you can start. You can ask your child if someone is hurt or did something break, revealing the urgency of a situation. This will help you evaluate what is going on with your child's situation. You must remain calm and encourage your child to remain calm. When restoring calm to your child, remember to validate the feeling they are having by stating its presence first. Example, "I see you're upset about this, but take a deep breath and tell me again what's going on in a nice voice. Then give them a chance to talk to you calmly. If it seems to be something dangerous, address it immediately and thank your child for letting you know. If it seems they are merely tattling on something. Continue with these tips:

If it turns out to be a simple case of, "he said, she said" and your child is in fact tattling, do not give in. Do not reward the tattling in any way. Instead, talk to the child that is tattling and find out why they are telling you what they are telling you. Then help all children involved to resolve it by working with them but don't resolve it for them. Ask them to suggest ways they think they can resolve the situation and give them all a chance to share their side of the story. Then work together to choose a better solution other than running to Mom or Dad. Guide them to understand that they can resolve these kinds of problems on their own. Talk to them about what they can do if a problem like this happens again. Do not get sucked into the drama. Your job is to calm the situation and then encourage the kids to learn how to resolve the conflict on their own.

It is always important to help your child understand the necessity of telling an adult or teacher if they see or are involved in a potentially dangerous situation. Teach them to recognize danger by recognizing when their tummies don't feel quite right. In addition, make it clear that disagreements between friends and siblings are best resolved between the kids involved. Let them know that if they share ideas with each other they can come up with a better way to do things and work together.

Thirty Four

"WHY?" THE MOST AGGRAVATING WORD IN A TODDLER'S VOCABULARY

The conversation goes something like this...

>Parent: "Please put your pants on."
>Toddler: "Why?"
>Parent: "Because you can't go to school in your underwear."
>Toddler: "Why?"
>Parent: "Because your legs will get cold."
>Toddler: "Why?"
>Parent (slowly losing patience): "Because it's cold outside."
>Toddler: "Why?"

Parent (about to explode): "BECAUSE I TOLD YOU TO AND IF YOU DON'T GET YOUR PANTS ON RIGHT NOW YOU ARE HEADING FOR A VERY LONG TIME OUT!!!!!!"

Sound a bit familiar? Have you had almost the exact same scenario in your house? Does the sound of the very first "Why" response make you cringe? Does your patience run out as soon as the "why's" begin?

You're definitely not alone. Toddlers have been asking "Why" in every language known to man since the beginning of time and parents have been exploding at their toddlers since the beginning of time in response to the non-stop "Why's".

So, what should you be doing different? Should you just take strong sedatives until the WHY stage passes? Should you just lock 'em away until they're older... hah!!! You may want to, but no, that is not only illegal, it won't solve anything.

Let's talk about the WHY in WHY. Why do toddlers ask that one-worded question over and over again that grinds on everybody's nerves? Why? Why? WHY?????!!!!!!!

Well, the real answer to that is... (drum roll please)... They're curious. They really want to know why.

Let's step back and put ourselves in your child's shoes. Imagine for a minute that you have only been alive about 2.5 to 3 years and about 8 months of that time you were for the most part, an infant. Now close your eyes and think about it. Too hard to imagine? OK, think about this. Imagine you have been blind your whole life and all of the sudden you wake up one day and you can SEE!! Or maybe you have been deaf your whole life and you wake up one day and you can HEAR... or TASTE... or SMELL. Now you're catching on. Exactly, you would want to see everything there is to see, hear everything there is to hear, taste everything there is to taste and smell everything there is to smell. You basically would want to learn about everything in your world. Well that is exactly what is going through the mind of that toddler of yours. They are learning about not just one or two things, they are learning about EVERYTHING and they can't learn fast enough.

Everything to them is new. Everything to them is something to touch, taste, see, hear and ask WHY about so they absorb all the information possible.

You did not give birth to a little adult, you gave birth to a baby. A little underdeveloped human, that with your help and guidance will become a developed, intelligent and well-adjusted adult (well, at least that is the goal).

Let's look at another example that may go a little better this time...

Parent: Please put on your raincoat.
Toddler: Why?
Parent: Because if you don't wear your raincoat your clothes will get all wet.
Toddler: Why?
Parent: Because it's raining outside. (Then show the child that it is raining)
Toddler: Why?

Parent (as the parent is putting the raincoat on their child): Because the sun dries up the water and the water forms clouds and the clouds get so heavy with water that the water falls down to the ground as rain. (short & sweet)

OR

If the parent doesn't know...

Parent: I actually don't know, so let's get into the car and head to school. When we get home you and I will look up why it rains so we can both learn about it together.

In this second scenario the parent tries to inform the child of what are the reasons while moving along with what needs to be done and ending the conversation with a "Let's go and we will learn later together" and not letting the toddler get the upper hand of the situation.

Here is another scenario and one that is one of my favorites and that you will find works exceptionally well.

> Parent: It's time to get into the car.
> Toddler: Why?
> Parent: Why do YOU think we need to get into the car?
> This will usually stop your child in their tracks and get them to pause and think.
> Toddler: Because we need to go to school.
> Parent: Correct!! Great job. Let's go.

In this third scenario, the parent actually turned the question around and asked the child to answer the "Why." Very often your child already knows why and they get in a habit of asking. So, when you know your child knows the answer, ask them to answer their own question. If they don't know the answer, then asking them, also gives them the opportunity to think about why something is happening. They may come up with a very logical answer all on their own.

The beauty of asking questions is that it always encourages conversation. Asking questions will come in handy as your child grows older and older. It is a way for you to find out more of what's going on in your child's life and vice versa. The more specific the question, the more specific the answer.

Getting aggravated with the whole thing solves nothing but creates agitation and anger for all of you. In addition, if you constantly stifle your child's curiosity and need to ask questions, you may inadvertently stop them from coming to you at all to ask any questions about anything in the future. Something you definitely don't want to happen.

Another way to limit the number of times your child says "Why" is with distractions or referring the conversation to later. It is perfectly ok for you to say to your child, "We don't have time right now to fully discuss this, but once we are back home (or finished whatever you're doing), we will sit down and really get some great answers to your questions."

You can also say, "Would you like to dance and start playing some music, or would you like to play a game, or help me fix dinner?" Distracting them from the "Why" cycle will also bring all the why's to an end in a calm, respectful, reasonable way.

Your child will always ask "Why." They will always want to learn more and that is ALWAYS a good thing. A curious mind is an intelligent mind. As their parent, your response will either encourage their curiosity in a controlled manner or it will make them realize that they should not be so curious and they will soon start keeping their thoughts and questions to themselves, therefore losing the desire to learn. You choose.

Thirty Five

TAMING THE TANTRUMS

Toddlers have been famous for throwing tantrums since the beginning of time. It's what they do. It's actually how they're wired. It's what drives most of us parents a little nuts. It's what we worry about when we are in public or at a social event--that at any minute our perfect angel might explode into a fury of uncontrollable emotion and we are left standing there, embarrassed, anxious, and stressed out, wanting it to stop and go away as soon as possible. So, let me set you on the right path right now. The solution is in your reaction. In fact, the solution is actually all about how you react, not how they react. You see, chaos breeds chaos, but calm breeds more calm. Let's talk about how you can control the situation. And the truth is you absolutely can control it and become pro-active so that your toddler's tantrums start happening less often and for a shorter length of time when they do occur. Sounds too good to be true, doesn't it? It's not. And you can do it too! I have coached many parents on how to react and almost eliminate tantrums from occurring as they travel through this emotional explosive stage. These tips, when applied, will do the same for you as long as you are consistent, and you don't lose your cool.

Here is the secret! When a tantrum happens remain calm, don't get upset, don't start yelling. Do not, and I mean, DO NOT give in to what they're having a tantrum about. Stay in control! You're the adult and being able to stay calm and in control is the difference between success and failure. If you don't think you have enough self-control, now is the time to work on building your patience and control. (Read Chapter 9 again)

If you give in to their tantrum and you give them what they want, you are only confirming that every time you say "no" or disappoint them in some way, they're going to have another tantrum. Why? Because it worked the last time, they threw one and they are pretty sure it will work again. So, stop giving them what they want when this outburst occurs and start teaching your child how to regulate their emotions. The next time they're disappointed, they can use the tools they have learned, to deal with it, think about it, and explore their options instead of having an explosion of raw, intense, screaming, kicking emotion.

Let's refer back to your child's brain for a minute. To put it simply, your child's brain is almost 100% pure emotions. They scream one minute; they laugh the next. To say their brain is underdeveloped is an understatement. All the self-regulation, the logic, the compassion, the "let's look at this realistically" stuff, is just not there. What is there however, is drastically in need of training and coaching. That's where you come in. In fact, that's your job as a parent. Your job is to develop the areas of self-regulation that your toddler so desperately needs, to coach, to teach, to guide. If you approach a tantrum with the same yelling and screaming that your toddler is doing, you are only confirming that this behavior is not only acceptable, it is the preferred and correct way you react to disappointment. If you approach the tantrum calmly and serenely, you give your toddler the opportunity to calm themselves down. They learn how to regulate the emotion that they are feeling at the time. Your child learns that they have the ability to start responding in more suitable and productive ways.

Let's discuss another important factor of when they're having a tantrum and that is the location of the tantrum. Why is location important? If your child is in the comfort and safety of your home, you should react one way. If your child is throwing their tantrum on a step or other potentially dangerous location in your home, then you will need to move them to safety. However, if your child is in the middle of a store with the happy public around them, you need to react differently.

First of all, let's talk about the safety of your home. When they are in a safe location during the time they're having their tantrum; be it their bedroom, your living room, etc., walk away and let them have their tantrum and then return once they've calmed down. If, however, when you walk away, this makes their tantrums worse, then just sit close by where they can see you while they get over the tantrum. Make sure even though you are close by, that you don't respond. Being near them allows your child to retain their feeling of safety and comfort. However, don't go overboard; don't react, don't cuddle or nurture to get them to calm down. Your child is having their tantrum because of their inability to self-regulate their emotions. Children are always yearning for their parent's attention. If you give them your attention during a tantrum, they will learn that this is a great way to get your attention and they will continue this behavior.

Next, do not yell and scream. When you yell and scream at them in response, they are just going to yell and scream right back. Think about being with an adult who's screaming and yelling. If your reaction is to yell back at them and respond in the same way they are, there's just more yelling going on and a screaming match ensues. It's the same with a child, if you are just continuing the yelling and the anger, the tantrum will never be resolved. They will just continue their frustration and yell and scream even more.

Remember that you're the grown-up and let them have their fit. Always recall my insistent reminder that they have little underdeveloped brains and they're all emotions. In contrast, your brain is developed, you're an adult, you can self-regulate. Your toddler cannot just yet. So, when they're throwing all these emotions at you-- they're throwing tantrums, then the next minute they're laughing-- that's because that's what they've got to work with. So, you have to allow them the time to work through that emotion without adding to it by losing your patience.

Once your child calms down, hug your child and love your child. This would also be the time to talk to them about what went on, after they have calmed down. Always tell them that you love them. Toddlers need to know that you love them regardless of how they are behaving. So, once you've calmed the situation and you've talked about it, (you've hugged, you've kissed), tell them you love them too.

Another great technique is to distract them. Distractions work great for many situations including tantrums. If they're throwing a fit, put on some music, make it loud, start dancing, throw out a bunch of balloons (it's a good idea to keep a bag of under-deflated balloons in a closet of your house) and before you know it that kid will be playing with you. You both will be having fun again.

Here's another fun tip. While your child is throwing a tantrum, sit in a chair close by and just continue to repeat, "I could sure use a hug. I wish someone would give me a hug." Repeat this loud enough for your child to hear and keep repeating it. Before you know it, that little angel will crawl over to you, crawl into your lap and give you a shy, wonderful little hug. You both will be relaxed and joyful and ready to continue with your day. I did this with my Grandson during one of his tantrums and it worked great and before I knew it, that sweet boy had crawled in my lap and melted into my arms.

Be aware of what triggers your child. The most common triggers for children are hunger, thirst, overwhelm and lack of sleep. So, if your child is in need of one of these things, then be pro-active and don't put them in a situation that will create a negative response. For example: Your child needs a nap, you know your child needs a nap, but you need to go to the store. No matter how badly you need to go to the store, you would be wise to give them a nap first. I guarantee you, if you choose to head out to the store without them having a nap, it is going to cause irritability and possibly accelerate into a tantrum. Another example, if they are hungry and you're trying to get them to clean up their room, they may be defiant, they're going to be irritable and a chance of a tantrum becomes a strong possibility. Think about when you're hungry or thirsty you get irritable, they do too. Remember, they're all human just like you! Wouldn't it be easier on everyone, if you just took a break and fed them, or let them sleep and then do what you need to do?

So, with a little observation, a little detective work and noticing when these tantrums happen, you can become proactive to alleviate them from happening in the future. Remember though, if you put them into a situation when they are in need of one of these triggers and you don't resolve the trigger first, you actually don't have the right to be upset with them when they lose control. You need to accept responsibility for their behavior if they lose it. You knew the risk and you chose to do it anyway. They just did what a tired child does and that is of no fault of their own.

Start taking action on these tips today and you will see a change in this behavior as your child learns to regulate their disappointment and their tantrums all on their own.

Thirty Six

AGGRESSION: TAMING THE MONSTER WITHIN

I hear it all the time and parent's see it all the time, the hitting, the biting, the kicking, the screaming, what's a parent to do? It's a stage that frankly keeps all of us on edge.

First, let's see why this happens. We need to understand why this happens before we can talk about how to stop it. Toddlers act out primarily due to their under-developed brains. Oh no, not back to the brain. Absolutely back to the brain because the toddler brain is so overrun with emotion and contains so little self-control or any understanding of what they should do when an intense emotion takes over. This inability to control themselves when they are overcome with confusion, anger, overwhelm or they're simply just mad at something, creates what's similar to a volcanic eruption of energy. This energy explosion will show up as a punch, a scream, a tantrum, a kick, a bite or any other lashing out that will help them release that emotion and pent-up energy. It is not your child being mean, it is not them taking it out on you. It is in fact just as I described it, an uncontrolled explosive response to all of that emotion.

So now that you understand their need to release, you may better understand how you can help teach your child how to regulate their reactions to those emotions.

- Being a pro-active parent will go a long way in helping your toddler understand and control their emotions. First of all, make sure you have routines in place for as many periods of the day as you can. (See Chapter 25: Schedules & Routines)

- Make time to spend one on one time with your child every day. Even ten to fifteen minutes can go a long way in changing the temperament of your child.

- Participate in social situations, like classes, play dates, etc., on a weekly basis if possible.

- Be sure to give your child boundaries and limitations so that their schedules and routines are carried out in a timely manner. Limit their use of items like tablets, television, video gaming and other electronics. Set timers if necessary.

- Exercise your child's disappointment muscle whenever it presents itself. After all, they need to realize in life, things don't always go your way. Exercise their waiting muscle as well, so they develop a strong understanding and ability to deal with delayed gratification.

- Allow for time spent outdoors in the fresh air. Fresh air is cleansing and rejuvenating and is a great way to calm anyone down from a tense situation.

- Talk about your emotions and how you handle them. Offer examples of what you have done when you have felt angry or overwhelmed. Read stories about working through your emotions and then discuss with your child what you have read to help them understand the story even further.

- Schedule in daily relaxation breaks with your family; yoga, meditation, prayer, reading, crafts, exercise, balloon play, Play-Doh®, clay, quiet music, outdoor walks, etc. All of these activities help to reduce everyone's stress.

- Notice and praise your child's positive behavior. Place more focus on noticing the positive and letting your child know that you have noticed and less time focusing on negative behaviors.

- Teach your child to count to five before reacting. Practice the 5 count together so it becomes automatic for them.

- Use reminders of how to play cooperatively and kindly before play begins with others. If your child has a playdate with a friend that often escalates into aggressive behavior, you may want to observe their play until you are confident that they can play kindly without aggression.

- Make sure all directions to your child are simple and offered one at a time. No general directions either. Ex: Do not say, "Set the table" instead offer step-by-step directions to a toddler… "please place these dishes in front of each chair, now put the napkins on the plates, now the forks on the napkins… etc. Be sure that all requests of your child are age appropriate.

- Allow your child to choose from two choices during negotiable situations. Ex: "What pair of pants would you like to wear, the green or the blue?" Giving your child choices where choices are available, empowers them and encourages them to cooperate more when choices are not available to them.

- Teach your child to express themselves through speech and confirm their feelings when they have them. Ex: "I see you're mad, however we cannot push your friends."

- Plan your consequences before the conflicts occur. What will you do if your child does continue to hit, bite or do some other form of negative behavior?

Now let's specifically address some of the most common aggressive behaviors demonstrated by toddlers and what your response to them should be to prevent continuing issues.

BITING

If they bite YOU… firmly say, "I will not let you bite me. Biting hurts." Remember that when your child is allowed to hurt and disrespect their parents without consequence, they will think it is ok for them to act this way towards anyone.

If they bite ANOTHER PERSON:

- Remove them from the situation, put them somewhere safe and tell them firmly, "I will not let you bite…"

- Then attend to the person that was bit and apply first aid if needed. Making sure they are ok.

- Then occupy the hurt child with something to do like coloring or books and go back to speak with your child and discuss what happened. If at this point your child is overly upset and having a tantrum, let him calm down, before speaking with him.

- When you speak to your child, speak firmly and clearly, eye to eye. Once things have calmed down and your child seems relaxed, bring them back to the person they hurt and have them apologize to them.

- Distract them if necessary, with another activity or if all seems calm and peaceful, allow them to play together again.

- If you're child bites a lot, you can offer them teething rings to bite on, cold cloths, foods that are chewy or harder to bite like celery, corn on the cob, carrots, bagels, etc.

HITTING

This is another common reaction to being angry or frustrated. If they are hitting you… try to catch their arm before they strike if possible and hold it firmly (not painfully) and tell them the same advice I gave you for biting and with a firm voice, looking them in the eye, "I will not let you hit me." Or "I will not let you hit… your brother, the dog, your friend (fill in the blank with the recipient of their anger)." Remove them from the situation and continue with the instructions above for biting.

You can also offer a toddler "a hitting pillow". Let me make this clear, this is not giving them permission to hit, instead this is giving them an outlet for their uncontrolled aggression until the time when they are able to regulate their behavior and create alternate ways to handle their emotions. And trust me, that time will come.

If you are worried that your child may hit or bite another child while playing together, your best defense is to stay close to them while they are playing so you can easily oversee what is going on and take control if it seems necessary.

THE STAC METHOD

If you find hitting, biting or other aggressive behaviors to be a regular occurrence, I recommend you take a week to completely observe your child when they are in these situations and complete the STAC METHOD CHART (a printable .pdf can be found on the website www.TamingTheToddler.com). If your child is under the care of another person, they should complete this chart as well.

The STAC Method is a way for you to observe your child, record their behavior and truly get a grip on when these behaviors are happening and what is triggering them. Common triggers are hunger, thirst, tiredness, being overwhelmed, control and attention.

STAC stands for S = SCENARIO, T = TRIGGER, A = ACTION, C = CONSEQUENCE

After the STAC Chart is completed, review it and find the common triggers and elements that you can take action on and work to prevent this continued negative behavior.

Here is an example of the chart.

The STAC METHOD
© 2019 Celia Kibler

Helping You Get Control Over Your Toddler's Aggression...
Tantrums, Biting, Hitting & other Explosive Behaviors.

The STAC Method is a way for you to observe your child, record their behavior and truly get a grip on what and when these behaviors are going on.

Please note: This observation technique is similar to those recommended by other doctors, therapists and care givers. I have broken it down into these 4 categories to help you really understand what is going on with your child, so that you can be pro-active in helping them deal with, understand and regulate their emotions.

Take a week, observe and record when your child's aggression happens and what the scenario is when it happens.

S = SCENARIO, **T** = TRIGGER, **A** = ACTION, **C** = CONSEQUENCE

SCENARIO	TRIGGER	ACTION	CONSEQUENCE
The SCENARIO includes: 1. Time of Day 2. What your child is doing (eating, playing with a friend or sibling, getting ready for bath, nap, etc. 3. Is there a specific person they're with when this happens? 4. Are they approaching sleeptime, mealtime? 5. Are they in a chaotic situation? i.e. play group, party, class, etc. 6. Are they playing with a certain toy or object?	The TRIGGER includes: 1. Hunger 2. Thirst 3. Need Sleep 4. Overwhelm 5. Having to share 6. Being told NO 7. Having to stop an activity, etc.	The ACTION is WHAT DID YOUR CHILD DO... 1. Hitting 2. Biting 3. Screaming 4. Tantrum 5. Throwing something 6. Spitting etc.	The CONSEQUENCE is what YOU HAVE IN PLACE when this behavior happens & how successful was the consequence? 1. Time Out 2. You told them not to do that 3. You bit or hit them back 4. You yelled at them 5. You did nothing wrong

NOW CREATE A SIMILAR CHART for you to use with the headings... S... T... A... C...
Everyday when you are with your child or your caregiver is with your child, ask them to record what is going on when the incident occurs.
You will begin to see a pattern that you can then take action on, so that you avoid the behavior from reoccurring.

Finally, I want to address what you should not do as a reaction to this aggressive behavior. Never call your child names or label them. (i.e.: my child is a bad boy, a biter, a hitter) or say things like "What is wrong with you?" Now you know that the problem is not with your child, but with the limitations of the toddler brain and the need for you to be pro-active and learn to stay calm in stressful situations, so that your child can learn self-regulation from you, their parents.

One more thing, never bite them back so "they know how it feels". You are just confirming the negative behavior and giving them permission to continue doing it. After all, if their parent can hit or bite, why can't they. Remember, your child will copy your behavior much more than your words.

Lastly, if the negative behavior happens between friends, do not force them to play together until the two are really ready to play nicely. Understand that this may not happen on the same day.. Watch and observe. Use your gut instinct; it's probably right.

Thirty Seven

POTTY-TRAINING: IT'S NOT JUST A JOB, IT'S AN ADVENTURE!

We all look forward to the day our child becomes diaper free and starts using the potty. Imagine the day you get to say, "Hooray, you did it! No more diapers!" Although as great as that feeling is, we are faced with the worry of how this potty-training thing will go.

The thought of potty-training includes thinking about all that comes with it... Accidents! Oh, but what about always having to make sure your child goes to the potty, the worry if you're out somewhere and they have to go and there is nowhere to go; or you what if they don't make it in time? It's kind of a love-hate relationship. The love of the thought of not having to buy diapers anymore and the hate of going through the process, as well as realizing your baby is growing up. It's a mixed bag of emotions for sure. I honestly believe potty training has more to do with training the parents, than it does the child. So, in this chapter I will address both, your fears and their ability to control what they have never had to worry about controlling before.

Through all of this, I want you to remember one important thing. That is, how many 20-year olds do you know that still wear diapers?

Unless they have a special need for a diaper, the majority of 20-year olds use the bathroom successfully day after day. I tell you this so that you can remind yourself that, one day, you and your child will be successful at this potty-training thing. There will be trials and tribulations, as there are with any change of behavior, but if you stick with it, stay consistent and follow the advice in this chapter, you both will achieve success.

Let's start with you. Yes, it is a lot easier to just put on a diaper or a pull-up and be done with it. If the pee or poo happens, we change it. Yes, it is a lot easier to just not think about it every minute of every day and go on about your business without the worry of their business. Yes, the struggle is real, the fears exist, but what's your alternative?

Let's face it, eventually your child will use a toilet in lieu of their pants. Your child will find their control and be able to "hold it" when needed. Yes, it really will be much easier once your child "gets it" and yes, the cost of diapers, which is substantial, will be removed from your life, (that is, at least, for this child).

Now let's discuss your fears. We all think this child will never get potty-trained, but the truth of the matter is, unless your child has a cognitive or physical challenge, they will succeed. Some may take longer than others, but, eventually, through your consistency and a few helpful strategies that we will discuss in this chapter, your child will make you proud, make themselves proud and go potty! It's exciting, it's curious, it's a challenge, but it can and will be done. All of us started in diapers and all of us ended up in underwear. The challenge is real, but so is the success!

Let's address this part of the path to raising successful grown-ups called potty-training. How will you do it? When should you do it?

What should you do if it's not working out so well? Keep in mind, there are many methods out there. You'll get advice from family, friends, different books and, of course, the advice I give you here. I will let you know that I have potty-trained my children, helped with my grandchildren and, at the writing of this book, my two year old grandson is mastering the art of going to the bathroom. The first thing I'll tell you is whatever method you decide to use, consistency is key. If you are not consistent, the potty-training will drag on and on. In addition, if you have multiple people caring for your child, grandparents, day care workers, etc., you ALL need to be on the same page with the methods used and the consistency in place across the board.

Now, let's go into the tips and methods that I recommend you use. The big question is when do you start? Again, you will find a range of opinions. Some people, like my mom, just begin when their child turns one. She didn't know you were supposed to wait and, for her, it worked. My sister was potty-trained by one. Sounds crazy, right? It's not and others have accomplished this feat as well.

My recommendation for when you should start is when your child shows an interest in the potty and recognizes that they have a dirty diaper. Your child may also start to sense the feelings of urination and/or bowel movements. This is a great time to start introducing the potty and usually begins around the time your child is approximately 18 months. In addition, when you do decide to potty-train your child, they should be having soft bowels and not be fighting any type of constipation. If your child is constipated, or has difficulty pooping, it will make going on the potty a challenge and could cause a lot of discomfort and frustration.

Most children are anywhere from about 18 months to three years when parents begin to focus on potty-training. Personally, I opt for starting closer to 18 months to two years. However, that is not the law and it varies a lot between children because we all develop at different stages. You can begin to encourage your child by helping them be aware of their body and the sensations they feel when they pee or poop. Start getting your child familiar with toilets by letting them watch you, (and their siblings if they have any), go potty, reading books about going potty and watching their favorite character talk about going potty, (Daniel Tiger[1] has many episodes that teach potty going concepts and acceptance). Discuss what is going on with their body, why they go to the bathroom and help them understand that every person and creature goes potty. As a bonus to encourage the process, let them choose their own special potty so it will be more personal and empowering for them.

Okay, your child seems ready. They want to sit on the potty, they want to flush it, they want to watch the poop or pee go down, they want to read books about it. Basically, they are showing you: I'm ready, so let's get going with going on the potty.

Here's where to start.

1. Make sure you are feeding your child a lot of healthy, fiber filled foods (fresh vegetables & fruit), and lots of water.

2. If you can go a week where your child stays in most days and is able to not wear a diaper or underwear, this will speed up the process. If not, no worries you can still get the job done.

3. Start taking your child to the potty frequently, every 30 minutes to an hour apart. Although you want to encourage them to let you know when they need to go, do not wait for them to tell you, they won't do this for a while. With that said, if and when they do tell you, even if it just after they went, take them so they understand the action of asking and getting results. After they are consistently going for a couple of weeks, you can start taking them hourly and as they get better and better every 2 hours. Once they get pretty good at telling you they have to go, you can begin to leave it up to them. However, if they have not gone for a few hours, you may want to encourage them to go. Trial and error will be the way you find the comfort spot for your child. Remember, it is not healthy to hold your pee for a long time, so encourage them to go potty more frequently.

4. If you have decided to offer rewards (see 5 in the Important Tip Section), it is important to incorporate it as soon as you begin potty training.

5. As I mentioned before, consistency is key! Once you have begun the process, don't stop. Potty training is full of trials, false alarms, mishaps and successes. However, if you say, "Oh I'll just put them in a pull-up today it will be easier", it may be easier that day, but it won't be easier in the long run. You are now contradicting all that you are trying to teach them in potty training. When you put a pull-up on them, you basically give them permission again to go in their pants.

6. Night Training: Some do it at the same time and some do it at a separate time after they have conquered the daytime. Either way works. I recommend you do daytime and then worry about the

nighttime. Regardless of whether you have started focusing on the nighttime, you should still get them used to going to the potty before bed and encouraging them to stay dry at night. Do not give them a lot to drink about an hour before bed. If they are thirsty just a sip or two will do. If you give them a full glass of water before bed, they are guaranteed to pee while they sleep.

Important Tips on Potty Training!

1. HAVE A POTTY SEAT ON EVERY FLOOR OF YOUR HOUSE & if needed in more than one room depending on how large your house is. You should at least have a potty seat in the rooms that are most commonly occupied by your family.

2. DON'T FORCE THE ISSUE BEFORE THEY'RE READY. This will only lead to frustration and a feeling of failure. Power struggles will result, and the potty will become an issue that your child actually avoids instead of accepts.

3. DON'T BE SHY, let them watch you. Your child yearns to be "big" and when they see the other members of the family using the potty, especially members of the same sex, they will be encouraged to use the potty and be a big kid too.

4. OFFER DISTRACTIONS. Help them relax when sitting on the potty. Read to them, tell stories of your own, sing songs or let them choose a toy they want to bring. If they have a doll, the doll can go potty too, after all, teamwork makes the dream work!

5. REWARDS. You can set up a reward system for when they go potty or even just sit on the potty and try. Make the reward

something fun or yummy. Chances are, if the reward is a slice of tomato, they will not be too encouraged to get one. Although I am not a huge advocate of eating a lot of candy, once in a while, it is not the end of the world. Often, parents will offer jelly beans or M&M's. I suggest one for peeing & two for pooping. A star sticker system works well too. Create a chart and buy different colored stars. When they try to go, but don't succeed, they get a blue star. When they pee, they get a red star and when they poop, they get a gold star, (or choose colors of your own). You can do it so they get to do something special for 3 gold stars. Talk to your child and set up your own system of what they get and when they get it. A reward can also be something like a trip to the park, playing ball, etc. Be creative and your child will get on board with going potty.

6. BE CALM: Accidents can and do happen. Have a change of clothes with you once they get potty-trained in case they slip up. Make sure you have wipes just like when they were in diapers. Don't forget socks! It also wouldn't be a bad idea to throw an extra pair of shoes in the car. When your child, (especially boys), have an accident, often the pee can reach their socks and shoes. NOTE: If you yell at them when they have an occasional accident, you will shut the process down and intimidate them. You will start creating more anxiety and stress which will lead to them having even more accidents due to their nervousness. Potty-training needs to be a pleasurable, not stressful, procedure and that includes the fact that they will have an occasional accident. You need to be okay with that.

7. OPINIONS: Don't let the opinions of others affect what you do or how you do. Stress, be it yours or theirs, will affect the process. Choose your method and stay the course. Be consistent and don't

determine your child's success based on some random deadline someone else determined. Your child will go potty based on your ability to stay calm. Work with them and encourage them. They will realize that they are big kids when they go potty and they no longer want to be a baby. Once they connect the sensation to the need to go, the magic will happen.

8. CLOTHING: Make sure the clothes that your child is dressed in are easy-on, easy-off. I recommend elastic waist not snaps & zippers. If your child can't get their pants off, they will have an accident to no fault of their own. Make it easy for them to go and they will.

There you go and now you're ready for them to go. I'll say it one more time so you don't forget (haha), consistency gets the job done!

- Don't give in!
- Don't put a diaper on because it's easier.
- Do put them in loose, easy-off clothes.
- Do take them to the potty on regular intervals to start.
- Do compliment their effort whether they go or not.

Remember, don't take any of it personally, it's not about you. It's about getting them to realize that there is a better option and that option it to go on the potty. They become a big kid. They take responsibility for their own body…and let's get real, it feels a lot better to put your poo in the potty than squishing it all over your butt. Go forth and conquer!!

---

1 Daniel Tiger's Neighborhood is an American-Canadian animated children's television series produced by Fred Rogers Productions, 9 Story Media Group, and Out of the Blue Enterprises.

Thirty Eight

BREAKING THE HABIT: PACIFIERS, BOTTLES OR WHATEVER ELSE THEY'RE ATTACHED TO THAT NEEDS TO STOP

Breaking a habit that your child has is never fun, but it's a fact of life. Your encouragement and consistency will get the task done.

All children are different. Some break habits easily and others have a more difficult time. For you, my advice is to stay the course. Just like the advice I gave you in Chapter 37 on potty-training, your determination to weather the storm will have this parenting job become a part of your past in a matter of days.

Unlike potty-training, breaking the bottle or pacifier habit is more up to you than your child. With potty-training, it's dependent on your child learning that the potty is where you go. For breaking the bottle and pacifier habit, it's more dependent on you and your willingness to stay focused on the ultimate goal.

When you decide to break a habit, be it a pacifier, a bottle, a blanket or whatever your child is attached to, choose a deadline to have the job complete. Prepare your child, relate it to how big they are now and give it some time.

Stopping anything cold turkey may work for some, but most kids break habits easily and smoothly with transition, time and consistency.

Be the most energetic, happy, proud person when your child finally starts to do the behavior that you are looking for. When your child drinks from a cup, or leaves their favorite blankie at home, compliment them and make a big deal out of it. As I've mentioned before, your child wants to please you and when they find something that they are doing that is making you happy, they will continue to repeat that same behavior.

Let's get specific for a minute on breaking Bottles and Pacifiers, as these are two of the most common habits that your child needs to grow from.

THE BOTTLE

Before eliminating the bottle, start introducing a cup so that your child has the opportunity to learn to drink from a cup before taking the bottle away. In this day and age of awesome inventions for kids, there are a myriad of cup choices out there. One of my favorite choices for a first cup is made by Munchkin®. Munchkin's trainer cups have large, easy to grip handles for little hands and soft silicone spouts. If you can't find this particular brand, there are many manufacturers that create a similar product. Watch your child because as soon as they can hold and maneuver their bottle, they can start using a cup. Straws are not something your child will know how to do the minute you offer one. However, through consistently offering it and some experimentation, they will, suddenly and accidentally, suck up the liquid. Once that occurs a couple of times, they have it figured out and they'll do it again and again.

Now that your child has mastered the cup, start offering their bottle less and less. By this point, they should have a cup with their meals at all times. During playtime, fill their cup with water and set the cup out for them to easily grab when they get thirsty.

By a year old, your child should transition from formula to milk and start using a cup. Once they are eating three good meals a day, like you and I do, their nutrition will come from their intake of food, making their formula, (basically a meal in a bottle), unnecessary. As a benefit, your costs are cut down a lot when you stop having to buy formula. Without formula, your child's need for a bottle becomes less and less.

If you are nursing, you can also start putting your breastmilk in a cup as well and start transitioning your child off the breast.

THE BEDTIME BOTTLE

Many parents continue offering a bottle before bed, due to the habit formed when your child was an infant. Parents tend to believe that their child will sleep better and longer if they have a bottle, (basically a meal), before bed. I respectfully offer that this is more of a habit, than truth.

Imagine eating a whole meal before bed; it's a lot. When you give your child an 8 oz. bottle before they go to sleep, that's basically what you are giving them. As an infant eats less often throughout their day, but, as a toddler who has enjoyed three complete meals and snacks during the day, their hunger is more than satisfied by bedtime. You can always offer your child a small snack between dinner and bedtime. Great snacks to offer at this time of night could be a few grapes and a small amount of milk or yogurt, oatmeal, a banana, berries, cereal, etc. Be sure not to offer your child sugary or caffeinated snacks and always brush their teeth after this evening snack to clean their mouth before bed.

At this point their need for sleep is much more of a priority than their need for yet another full meal. If your concern for your child is their thirst, then a small cup filled with a little water is all your child needs before falling to sleep. In addition, when it's time to potty train your child at night, you are not having the added challenge of a full belly of liquid that their bladder will need to get rid of in a few hours. Break the nighttime bottle now, when they're about a year old, it's unnecessary and it will save you a lot of headaches in the future.

THE MIDDLE OF THE NIGHT BOTTLE

After about 6-7 months of age, your child should be sleeping well throughout the night. If at this point they wake up wanting a bottle, it is more the habit of wanting to see you than an actual issue of hunger. If they have eaten well throughout the day and have remained active and stimulated, they should be sleeping through the night without the extra meal. If they are breastfed, this may not be the case and you may have to wait longer before eliminating the mid-night feeding. You will know when they are ready to skip this feeding all together when they wake up, see you, get a bottle or the breast, drink for a few minutes and then fall right to sleep again. I recommend that you try alternative ways to soothe them to break this habit of waking in the middle of the night. If they wake up, give them a chance (about 5 minutes) to fall back to sleep on their own before going in to see them. If they still do not fall back asleep, go in and sing to them and rub their back, top of their head or forehead to relax them. Refrain from picking them up. This will usually do the trick and they will fall back asleep. However, if you have tried all of this and they are still not asleep you can try picking them up and rocking them. If you need to offer them a bottle again as you break this habit, put less and less liquid in the bottle each time it is offered. You can also start thinning out their formula or milk with water as you start reducing the amount of liquid in their nighttime bottle.

PACIFIERS, WUBBIES, BINKIES...

You name it, it's time to break the habit. There are lots of schools of thought out there on breaking the binky habit and all of them work for some people; none of them work for all people. So, you will have to try and figure out what works best for you and your child.

1. There's the "this ends today" method or simply going "Cold Turkey". That's when you choose a day, stick to it and the binky is gone. With this method like most of the others, you will soothe your child's sadness for the loss of the binky in other ways. But be consistent and in a few days, your child will sleep like a lamb. Also make sure there are no pacifiers just laying around the car or house in areas that your child can find them.

2. There is the "Gradual to Gone" method. One I particularly like. I feel like it is a bit less stressful for your child. Plan a day for the pacifier to be removed but lead into that day gradually. End the traveling pacifier first. No more car rides with it. No trips to the store with it. The pacifier stays in the house and the house only. After a couple days of house only pacifier, then it becomes the bed only pacifier. In short, it never leaves the bedroom and is only used at nap and bedtime. After about a week, it is no longer available at naps and only at bedtime. Then set you date, a few

days, a week later, a month later, whatever you choose, write it on the calendar and end it. The pacifier is gone on that date. Talk about it with your child, prepare for it and then it's over. Options for the end... bury it, cut the tip so it's damaged and your child will eventually not want it anymore. Mail it or drop in a donation bin for a baby that needs it (let your child do this with you). I have even heard of someone using it for the child to paint pictures and then the pacifier was a mess and the child rejected it on their own.

3. Let me start by saying DO NOT USE HOT SAUCE! I had hot sauce put on my thumb to stop me from sucking my thumb and it was horrible!!! I hated it. Honestly, I think my mom hated doing it too, but she did that as a last resort. After using the hot sauce, I will tell you, I still sucked my thumb and I was left with horrible memories of hot sauce. You can rub things like very minty toothpaste, mouthwash, mustard, coconut oil, etc. Be creative, but make sure it's yucky enough that it discourages your child from wanting it in their mouths. Make sure anything you put on their pacifier is perfectly safe to eat.

Choose the way you want to do it and it will be done. Don't give in, once you decide it's gone, be prepared for their loss and know that the sadness won't last forever. There are lots of children's books about breaking the pacifier habit too that you can read to your child to help them understand and prepare for the big day.

Consistency, compassion, understanding, creativity and love will get all of you through this stage. It will result in your child breaking the habit that you have targeted. It can be done. Thousands of toddlers every day are breaking one habit or another.

I'll end with this question to help with your confidence that it can be and will be done. Do you know any 20-year olds that still use a binky?

Thirty Nine

SLEEP: MAKING IT HAPPEN

Sleep is one of those things that your child either does well or they don't. Many parents I work with will say my child's head hits the pillow and they are out. Other parents will tell me: I lay there in bed with my child, waiting for them to drift off and, before you know it, I'm sound asleep and they're still awake. Even after I wake up, 20 minutes later, and think they must be asleep by now, I look over and their eyes are wide open. What can a parent do? How do you get your child to sleep?

I feel like the best place to start this discussion is to tell you about sleep. There are stages of sleep we all go through, hopefully, to reach a night of rest. So, let's understand what those stages are in brief.

Stage 1: Is when you're so sleepy, you fight to stay awake. You see videos of kids doing this all the time and I'm sure you have seen your own child fighting sleep. Children's heads are bobbing, falling into oatmeal, sitting in a chair and falling over sound asleep. We've all seen it and we've all been there.

Stage 2: Light sleep that is heading for dreamland.

Stage 3: Deep sleep. This is where you get great rest and are totally relaxed. If someone wakes you up, you're groggy, disoriented and people know you were asleep.

Stage 4 REM SLEEP: (Rapid Eye Movement) This is where our dreams happen. In REM sleep your brain is working overtime, but your body is totally not.

As children grow from babies to toddlers to school age, they move from about a 50/50 split of NREM Sleep, (stages 1-3), and REM sleep to more time spent in NREM and less in REM. Without getting into too much science, just know that a child needs a good night's sleep to help their growth, as well as their cognitive development.

Here is a general idea of how much your child should be sleeping each day in relationship to their age. Notice that there is not an exact length of time as this will differ per child. We all require differing amounts of sleep, but this guide offers you a range for your child's age.

0-3mos.	10.5-18hrs./day
4-11mos.	12-16hrs./day
1-2yrs	11-14hrs./day
3-5yrs	11-13hrs/day
6-13yrs	9-11hrs/day

Now, let's talk for a minute about what can cause your child not to sleep well or have difficulty falling asleep. Afterwards, we will talk about what you can do to make sleep happen. Note that many of these tips apply to adults as well as children. If you want to sleep better as well, follow these tips.

Here are 6 outside stimuluses that can affect your child's sleep.

1. The Food or drink they have had throughout the day and within 6 hours of sleep. You need to avoid caffeine and sugars, heavy fried foods. Eat more healthy fruits and vegetables as well as grilled, baked or roasted meats and proteins.

2. The lack of a sleep routine. We will address this in what you can do to help with sleep.

3. Sudden changes in the environment. A new home, a new room, a new baby, a new school, even a parent having a new job and a change of work hours or daylight savings time. What might seem like a minor change to you can be a monumental change for your child.

4. Illness and medication.

5. Visitors to the house and excessive noise.

6. The anxiety from separation from their mom, dad or caretaker. Know that all children are different and situations may affect them in a myriad of ways.

7. Lack of activity throughout the day. If your child is spending a lot of time sitting and watching a screen, they're body doesn't get tired.

What can you do to be pro-active and help your child get into a better sleep routine and be ready to sleep when the time comes?

Here are 10 ways you can help your child get to sleep and stay asleep.

1. Bedtime routine. A bedtime routine is vitally important, and I can't stress this enough.

Your bedtime routine for your child should begin at least an hour before their "lights out" time. You see, your brain actually has the ability to know when it is time to settle down and go into "sleep mode". When you have a solid bedtime routine, it sends a direct signal to your brain that now is the time to start relaxing and get ready for a deep sleep. Here's an example of a bedtime routine:

6:30	Brush Teeth
6:45	Bath-time
7:00	get into pajamas
7:10	pick out clothes for tomorrow
7:20	pick out books to read before bed
7:25	read books
7:45	sing a bedtime song, talk a little together, give hugs and kisses
7:55 - 8:00	Lights out

   a. White Noise: a fan running is great for this & also keeps the room cooler, which is also important for sleep
   b. Bed is full of fluffy blankets, pillows and favorite stuffed animal(s)
   c. Room is mostly dark. A night light is fine but one that is not too bright.
   d. No electronics are on. No TV, tablets, etc.

2. Choose a wake-up & bedtime and keep it consistent every day, even weekends.

3. Naps should not be too close to the time they go to bed. Give 2.5-3 hours from the time your child wakes up from an afternoon nap, to the time they go to bed for the night.

4. Eat well throughout the day. Include healthy foods and avoid sugars and white flours as much as possible. Enjoy lots of fruits and vegetables.

5. Lots and lots of activity during the day. If a child sits watching a tablet all day are they exercising? No. In order to sleep well, one must be active to get tired. So keep them busy, keep them running around and they will be happy to reward you with a good night's sleep.

6. There are different ways to relax your child before lights out. If you go to the website, www.tamingthetoddler.com, you will find The Body Relaxation in the resources section. You can also find it in the Files section of the Facebook group BeABetterParent.com. This quiet relaxation will help your kid fall asleep and rest. Playing very soft classical or jazz music in their room can help as well.

7. Always say good night to them and let them know that you will see them in the morning. If you will not be the one that they'll be with when they wake, let them know who will be with them in the morning.

8. But, what if your child is usually a great sleeper and, suddenly, they have difficulty sleeping? Maybe they can't go to sleep or

maybe they are waking in the middle of the night. Take the time to find out why. It will usually have to do with illness, food intake, dreams, nightmares or a change in the routine. Be observant and ask them how they're feeling if they can talk and tell you. Check to make sure they don't have an upset stomach or fever. If you have found no reason for the change, be consistent each night as you work to get them back on their schedule. Reach out to me if you really can't figure it out.

Let me give you an example and share a story with you about my daughter. Lauren was always a great sleeper, two hour naps twice a day and 12 hour nights, the perfect child. All of a sudden, at about eight months old, Lauren decided her new bedtime would be 11pm, not her normal 7pm. I was like, "Oh no, that is not happening. That is past my bedtime."

So, after making sure nothing was wrong with her and recognizing that she just did not want to go to bed, I needed to do something to get her back on her schedule. Here's what I did. Every night, I put Lauren to bed a half hour earlier from 11pm until we were back on schedule to our 7pm bedtime. Yes, it took about a week; yes, she cried each night for about 5-10 minutes before she fell asleep; yes, it was hard and a bit stressful, but I was determined to get her back on schedule and my consistency paid off. In about a week, she was back on her nighttime schedule

9. Please, just "One More"? If you don't eliminate that phrase, your child will one more you to death. When they say one more book, one more song or one more sip of water, whatever it is, reply with:

"I'm sorry honey, but we have read your books, you had some

water and now it is time for you to sleep. I will see you in the morning." You can add, "I will check on you in a little bit," as well if you like, but that "little bit" should be about 20 minutes later

10. Do not keep going in and checking on your child every five minutes because you are not giving them a chance to fall asleep. Every time you check on them, you disturb the process. So, just one time is sufficient. If you have a video monitor, you can see your child and check on them. You can also address their needs if they want to talk to you through the audio of the monitor without walking into their room

For more sleep help, visit www.PumpedUpParenting.com and check out the available Sleep Training Videos

Here's to a good night's sleep, for all of you.

Forty

IT'S TIME TO TALK ABOUT IT: OPENING UP ABOUT DIFFICULT TOPICS

ANTI-RACISM

According to the Anti-racism Digital Library, "Anti-racism can be defined as some form of focused and sustained action, which includes inter-cultural, inter-faith, multi-lingual and inter-abled (i.e. differently abled) communities with the intent to change a system or an institutional policy, practice, or procedure which has racist effects." (Wikipedia)

So how do you get the message of Anti-Racism across to your toddler? Well, this chapter will help you do just that.

We live in a world where everyone is different, believes different things and comes from different cultures that influence the way they live. Honestly, who wants to live in a world where everyone is the same? It would be like a world of robots. Instead, humans come in all kinds of shapes and sizes. Various colors and features like noses, eyes, mouths, ears, hair and skin tone. Some people are tall, some short, some wear glasses or braces, some have crutches or wheelchairs, while others speak different languages with different accents. Humans come in different genders and fall in love with a different gender than their own or, sometimes, the same gender.

We all are different in one way or another, but we are all the same species–human. Remember, as your child meets people in your family, your neighborhood, and your community, they will notice things. For example, if you have two blocks and one is yellow and one is blue, you may ask your child which is the blue block and they may pick up the yellow one. At this point, most parents would correct them and point out the difference in the two colors. This is to help you realize that, just as your child sees the difference in two blocks, they will also notice the differences between themselves and another person. So, don't be surprised if they say to you, while standing next to a friend,

"Why is Amber's skin white?" or "Why is Joey's skin brown?"

They may ask about someone else's hair, glasses, wheelchair or ask why they don't celebrate Christmas. The point is, your child will notice differences, not in a rude, prejudiced way, but in an innocent, curious way. Your reaction to these questions tells all.

First of all, the worst thing you can do is to hush your child or say: "Don't ask that, you'll hurt their feelings."

Being curious and wanting to learn is not rude at all. In fact, it's a good thing. In my opinion, if adults would take more time to learn about each other, they would be less likely to prejudge or assume. This is true when parenting too.

What you should be doing is encouraging the questions by responding with the truth. Remember though, if you don't know the answer, let your child know that you don't know and do some research. If your child is old enough, then do the research together. Honestly, if your child is old enough to ask a question, they are old enough to look through books and learn new things.

As I have talked about throughout this book, they are learning mostly from you at this age. You are your child's strongest role model. To summarize–what you do, they will do; what you say, they will say. The way you communicate is the way they will communicate. It's a simple case of Monkey See, Monkey Do.

Which brings us to talking about the not so easy topics. You know, the topics that you procrastinate about, the ones you think, "Well, I will wait 'till they're older".

The truth of the matter is, if you don't talk about it, some random friend, another adult that you may not agree with, or even worse, the internet will. We live in a time of information, good or bad. It's all out there and available for anyone that wants to find it and, one day, that will be your child.

Even though your child is little, it is still important to start a conversation about the difficult stuff that we sometimes hesitate to talk about. That conversation needs to begin now, age-appropriately of course.

Let's first analyze the word "prejudice". It stems from Pre- and judging, what you should never do to your child and what you should never do with other people that you don't personally know.

In the movie "Remember the Titans", a true story about a Virginia high school in the midst of the Civil Rights Movement, the school's football team was, all of a sudden, due to bussing, a mix of whites and blacks, and suddenly coached by a black man. What ensued was conflict, anger and disbelief at what was taking place. The coach had to come up with a way to get this team to work and play together. He instructed every player to sit down with a player of the opposite race and get to know them, their family and what they liked. This eventually led to the team enjoying each other's company and truly becoming a brotherhood of men with a single goal: to make this team be the best to ever hit the field. This, of course, is a general overview of the movie. My point is, he had his team actually talk to each other to discover how similar they were once you took skin color out of the picture.

The reason I bring up this reference is to remind you that you need to be talking to your child about the differences that all humans present. Discuss people's differences and their similarities. For a toddler, our similarities break down to one head, one face, one body, two arms and two legs, etc. Don't think your child is not going to notice someone's skin color or hair color; they will, just like they notice the difference between a yellow block and a blue one. It's not racism for a child, it's curiosity and the innocence of trying to learn. So, talk to them about why people are the way they are and avoid hushing them. Your child's curiosity deserves your answers and avoiding it won't make it go away. Why does someone have dark or light skin?

Because their parents had similar skin and, when they were born, they looked a lot like their mommy and daddy. Then, show your child how they have similar features to you. That is the simple truth about why we all look the way we do, genetics.

When choosing dolls, and other toys for your child that model humans, be sure to choose a variety of ethnicities so your child becomes familiar with realizing that we do not all look the same. Don't just get white dolls because your child is white, black dolls because your child is black, Asian dolls because your child is Asian, etc. Allow your child's make-believe world to mimic the real world that we all live in every day.

Who are you and your child associating with? Do you live in a community that is made up of a variety of cultures and religions? Do you make it a habit to teach your children about different holidays that are celebrated by people around the world or do you just focus on your holidays, leading your child to believe that your lifestyle is the only one that exists?

Instead of creating a world where everyone is the same, try showing your child how fun and refreshing it is to live in a society where everyone is a little different. The old saying that variety is the spice of life is absolutely true.

Talk with your child about how you and their other parent are different or how they are different from a sibling, a cousin or one of their friends. Then, start exploring how they are the same. Maybe one wears glasses, one is in a wheelchair or one is of different skin color, hair color or religion. You can even show them how humans are different from animals, like your pets. If you have a fish, they are different because they live in water and have fins instead of arms and legs, but they are similar because fish have two eyes, one mouth, and need to breathe just like people. The point is, everyone and everything on this earth has differences and similarities. That's what makes life interesting and, frankly, better.

THE SEX TALK

What?? I have a toddler; don't tell me you want me to talk about sex already?

Well, in a way, yes. We are not going to get into the details of how babies are made, but this is a great time to talk about the differences in bodies and what makes someone a girl and what makes someone a boy. Simple biology.

This is also a great time to start introducing how your child's body belongs to your child and is a 'no' zone to other people. Teach your child that private areas are private, not for public display.

Although it may seem funny to your family, yanking down your child's pants for fun, especially in front of other people, it is actually anything but funny. It gives permission to your child to not only do that publicly to others, but to feel it is ok to expose private areas to the public. In other words, you are sending a mixed message that can cause confusion. This is an area of privacy that should have no confusion. It is off-limits to others and you should be teaching your child, even your toddler, to say NO when something just doesn't feel right or makes their belly feel funny, (a great way to explain to children what it feels like if something is off in a situation).

If your child asks you, "Where do babies come from?" Don't lie and tell them the vegetable garden or a stork. Also, don't give them a step-by-step of how a baby is conceived either; this can be confusing and scary to a toddler. There is a very simple way of explaining:

"When two people are in love, they decide they want to have a baby. They talk about it, laugh about it, dream about it, hug, kiss and love about it until the woman becomes pregnant and a baby grows in her belly, just like you grew in mine."

Then, show them pictures of when you were pregnant and when they were born. If a child is adopted, you can add to that story to include adoption. Read age-appropriate stories about where babies come from. Be realistic about the names of a penis and a vagina, but you don't need to go into all of the details of conception. It will be way over their head and that is something that can be taught down the road.

GENERAL ADVICE

Here are some tips about having difficult conversations with your kids and getting started at toddler age.

1. **START NOW.** The ability to talk about difficult subjects with your child and not avoiding questions they ask will lead you on an open road of communication as they grow. Your child will know that they can come to you for their answers to whatever is challenging them and you will become more and more comfortable talking about it.

2. **KINDNESS.** When you raise a kind child, compassion, understanding and respect will follow.

3. **EDUCATE.** Create an environment of learning new things in your home. Read stories on the topics you are talking about and discuss with them what they have read.

4. **BE A ROLE MODEL.** (Chapter 3) How you act, is how your children will learn to act. The way you live your life, the people you hang around with, the values that you hold true will be shared by your child as they grow.

The blessing of being human is that we all have a brain and a heart to use. It allows us to learn, create, discuss, react, understand our emotions and, most of all, love. By showing your child your compassion, education, respect, integrity and your ability to make up your own mind and believe your own beliefs, you give your child the understanding and ability to do the same. Be a good listener at all times. Don't be afraid to ask and don't be afraid to offer answers. Be willing to say you don't know and that you need to do more research. Calm, open communication is key.

IT'S NOT THE END, IT'S JUST THE BEGINNING

I know all the information in this book might seem a bit daunting, overwhelming and confusing. I want to give you a little tip: If you feel in your heart that something is not right, it's probably not. Go with your heart. You know your child better than anyone; trust your instincts. If you make a mistake, (and we all do), it doesn't make you a bad parent. If you need help, (and most parents do), reach out, talk about it with your partner, your family, your friends or reach out to me; that's what I am here for.

Take the tips in this book and try one or two at a time. Don't try to put in place everything you have learned all at once. Doing that may lead to complete overwhelm and failure. Step by step, tip by tip and before you know it, you have created your new life of peace and harmony with your family.

This journey you are on with that precious child of yours, is just the beginning. What you do today, what you teach them today, will reward them and you for years to come.

The seeds you plant now, will be the values, beliefs and behaviors that they take with them into adulthood. Realize that you are not raising children, you're raising adults and like anything that is worth doing, there will be challenges and struggles along the way but there will also be huge rewards. The biggest reward will be seeing the child that you created, supported and guided, become an adult that is reaching their maximum potential and enjoying a happy life. I see it every day when I look into the eyes of my adult children. Nothing makes a parent more proud or smile bigger.

These first 5 years are the most important. It's when your child learns their core values, their knowledge of right from wrong, their understanding of behavior, their ability to self-regulate, their limitations, boundaries, independence and emotional development.

They develop mad skills; physical, cognitive, social and language skills. They learn faster at this time in their life than at any other time. What you model, how you teach, and what you say are the behaviors that they will learn and the life lessons they will rely on for all the years to come. These skills they gain in these first 5 years is what will guide them through the rest of their life.

Plant your seeds well, water them, nourish them, nurture them and, before you know it, what will stand before you is the tallest, strongest, happiest tree in the forest. Your child, that miracle that you gave birth to, has become a truly miraculous adult.

Trust the process, trust yourself, trust your child and treasure every moment--the good, the bad, even the ugly, because that moment won't be back again and, in the blink of an eye, your baby will be all grown up.

Don't worry or stress about mistakes; they don't make you a bad parent, they make you human.

Enjoy the journey; enjoy life!

It's been an absolute honor and a pleasure sharing this journey with you. I hope you have taken action on all that you have learned within these pages.

CONTINUE YOUR JOURNEY... YOU'RE ONE SHIFT AWAY

Thank you for reading this book and for choosing to grow as a parent. Your willingness to learn, reflect, and shift old patterns is a powerful gift to your child, and to every generation that follows.

Your journey doesn't end here.

This is where your transformation deepens.

Below are the resources designed to support you as you create more cooperation, confidence, and connection in your home, one shift at a time.

1. Join the BeABetterParent.com Membership & Community

Your membership includes the full **Be A Better Parent App and access to our Skool community**.

Choose the level of support that fits your family:

Basic Membership

Includes:

- Full access to the **Be A Better Parent App**
- Access to the Skool community
- All free Skool trainings, lessons, and community resources
- A growing library of everyday parenting tools

Ideal for parents wanting steady guidance, reliable tools, and a supportive community.

Pro Membership

Includes **everything in Basic**, PLUS:

- All **Pro-Level Trainings**
- **Group Coaching & Q&A (**twice monthly**)**
- **Hot Seat Coaching** (once monthy)
- **Live Monthly Masterclass**
- Access to **premium workshops**, advanced trainings, and the full course library

Ideal for parents ready for ongoing coaching, deeper transformation, and step-by-step support.

JOIN THE MEMBERSHIP.
Scan to explore membership levels and begin your next step.

2. Be A Better Parent App

Your membership includes full access to the Be A Better Parent App. Your calm, confident parenting partner that goes wherever you go and whenever you need help.

Inside the app you'll find:

- Instant solutions for behavior challenges
- Scripts that build cooperation and connection

- Emotional regulation tools for both you and your child
- Quick mindset resets for overwhelming moments
- Practical strategies grounded in 40+ years of experience
- Support is now only one tap away, anytime you need it.

"DOWNLOAD THE APP"

3. Work Privately With Celia Kibler, the award-winning author of this book founder of BeABetterParent.com

Parenting support isn't just for the toddler years.

No matter the age or stage of your family, private coaching provides personalized guidance tailored to your unique needs.

Choose from four specialized coaching pathways:

- **Pregnancy to Infancy: Calm Beginnings**

Build a peaceful, confident foundation from the very start.

- **Raising Respect: Creating a Respectful Home without the Need to Yell or be agressive**

Support for all parents of children from toddlers through teens seeking cooperation, confidence, and calm communication and family harmony.

- **Peaceful Pathways: Two Homes, One Family, One Future**

For families navigating separation, divorce, co-parenting, or blending families with intention and stability.

- **The Family Reset: Seniors Older Parents**

For parents wanting healing, reconnection, and harmony with their adult children.

Wherever your family is right now, you are **one shift away** from meaningful change.

APPLY FOR PRIVATE COACHING

A Note from Celia

Thank you for being here.

Thank you for choosing compassion when it's hard, connection when it's messy, and intention when old patterns try to pull you back.

Your willingness to grow is already transforming your child's world.

Remember:

You're one shift away from a calmer home, a deeper bond, peace of mind and a child who feels truly seen, valued, and loved.

I'm honored to walk this journey with you.

~ Celia

ABOUT THE AUTHOR

Celia Kibler is a pioneer in family wellness, founder of BeABetterParent.com, and creator of the transformative Be A Better Parent App. With over 43 years of personal parenting, 30 years successfully parenting a blended family, and over four decades of professional and educa-tional experience, Celia brings unmatched real-world wisdom to every family she serves. As President of the Day of Calm Foundation, she leads a global movement to end yelling, shame, and violence against children, so we start raising generations of adults that don't have to recover from their childhood. Through her books, coaching, and nonprofit work, she empowers families to create peaceful, respectful homes where children and parents can truly thrive.

A Childhood That Sparked a Global Mission

Celia grew up with deeply loving parents, yet her father, recovering from his own abusive childhood, struggled with anger, a short temper, and verbal outbursts. Although he never physically harmed his family, the yelling and name-calling created an environment that shaped Celia's early beliefs about herself. It taught her to be non-confrontational and contributed to challenges in her early relationships, including the end of her first marriage.

Still, she always knew she was loved. She inherited her mother's optimism and compassion, her father's humor, and her family's shared love of music and entertainment.

At age 12, Celia was diagnosed with scoliosis and fitted for a full body brace that she wore from 8th through 12th grade. Monthly visits to Baltimore's Children's Hospital, located next to the terminal ward, gave her a profound and early understanding of gratitude, perspective, and resilience. She learned that no matter her struggles, someone else was facing a greater challenge. This mindset would become the backbone of her teachings and her life's work.

The negative beliefs planted in her childhood, "not good enough," "not capable," "not worthy", later fueled her mission: **to end the generational cycles of yelling, shame, fear, and emotional harm that silently persist in so many homes.**

Her guiding principle, "We are raising adults, not children," reflects her belief that the choices parents make today shape the adults their children will one day become.

Over 43 Years of Parenting Experience:

Real, Raw, and Relatable

Celia's greatest joy is her family. She is the mother of five grown children, two by birth and three through her blended family, and a proud grandmother of nine. She has over **43 years of real-life parenting** and more than **30 years raising a blended family**, giving her unmatched firsthand experience in navigating the complexities of modern family life.

Paired with over **40 years of professional and educational experience**, Celia brings a powerful combination of research, training, and real-world wisdom to her work. The strategies she teaches are not theoretical, they are lived, tested, and proven in the heart of family life.

Parents trust her because she has lived what she teaches.

Her methods work because they are built on experience, compassion, and practicality.

It is this authenticity that has earned her the title many parents use lovingly:

"The Baby Whisperer."

Leading a Global Movement to End Violence at Its Roots

Celia is the President of the Day of Calm Foundation, a 501(c)(3) nonprofit dedicated to stopping violence at its roots through intentional parenting, calm communication, and worldwide education. She leads impactful initiatives including:

- The **International Day of Calm** on April 5th and the accompanying 3 day Summit
- The **Rescue-a-School Initiative**
- Global parent education campaigns that equip families with tools to reduce yelling, conflict, and emotional harm in the home

Her mission is simple and powerful:
To create future generations of confident, kind, respectful adults by transforming the homes and hearts of the parents raising them today.

Media & Recognition

Celia has been featured on FOX News (NY & DC), CBS affiliate WUSA 9, in the Associated Press, The Washington Post, The Baltimore Sun, and numerous national and international media outlets. Her lifelong work spans teaching, coaching, public speaking, curriculum development, nonprofit leadership, and the design of tools that help families thrive, most notably the Be A Better Parent App.

Connect With Celia

Website & App: www.BeABetterParent.com

Day of Calm Foundation: www.DayOfCalm.org

Email: celia@BeABetterParent.com

Funfit® Family Fitness: www.Funfit.com

Social Media: YouTube • Facebook • Instagram • LinkedIn • Pinterest • TikTok

www.ingramcontent.com/pod-product-compliance
Lightning Source LLC
Chambersburg PA
CBHW070546160426
43199CB00014B/2396